THE WRITING BOOK

KATE GRENVILLE

THE WRITING BOOK

A Workbook for Fiction Writers

Allen & Unwin

© Kate Grenville 1990
This book is copyright under the Berne Convention.
No reproduction without permission. All rights
reserved.

First published in 1990
Fourth impression 1991
Allen & Unwin Pty Ltd
8 Napier Street, North Sydney, NSW 2059 Australia

National Library of Australia
Cataloguing-in-Publication entry:

Grenville, Kate, 1950–
    The writing book : a workbook of fiction writers.

    Bibliography.
    ISBN 0 04 442124 9.

    1. Fiction — Technique. 2. Fiction — Authorship. I. Title.

808'.3

Typeset in 10.5 pt Palatino by SRM Production Services, Malaysia
Printed by Southwood Press Pty Limited
80–92 Chapel Street, Marrickville, NSW 2204

for Woolfie

Introduction

T HIS isn't yet another 'how to write' book. In fact it
isn't a 'how to write' book at all. This is a practical
workbook, a resource book for a writer to work
through, with an emphasis on exercises and examples.

One of the basic philosophies behind the book is that our
minds are capable of much more than we usually think. For
most areas of our lives, we need our brains to be organisation
machines: in order to function, we train our brains to sort
out the relevant from the irrelevant, to put data in order of
importance and to work things out logically. That means
that a lot of our minds' other capabilities aren't called on so
often: the instinctive, intuitive ways of thinking that have
nothing to do with logic.

However, writing is one human activity that seems to
respond better to well-developed intuition than well-
developed logic. What this book tries to do is to give those
under-developed areas a chance to practise. At the same
time, it provides a carefully worked-out structure so that the
writer can safely explore aspects of the writing process in a
very open-ended way, knowing that there's a strong structure to return to.

The other basic philosophy behind this book is that
writers can start with what they already have and then
build from there. Anything at all can form the raw material
for fiction: any kind of experience and any kind of word-

use. You don't have to learn to be someone else in order to write fiction and you don't have to learn to speak with someone else's voice. What this book shows you is how to take whatever you already have and turn it inside-out and put it back-to-front in many different ways. This gradual process of transformation is the process of turning life into fiction.

It's more and more difficult now to draw a precise dividing line between fiction and other kinds of writing, and it's not very useful to try to do so. For practical purposes, what I mean in this book by 'fiction' is writing that isn't limited to real events, though it might make use of them: writing that is free to make things up if it suits its purposes. Much of this book would be very useful for writers of poetry or drama, but its focus is on prose narrative.

Fiction comes in many sizes: a piece of fiction can be one sentence, a story of a dozen pages, or a novel.

Fiction also comes in many shapes: some pieces of fiction take the shape of a traditional story, with a beginning, middle and end. Others don't tell a story, but structure the material around some other concept. Some stories aim to be so convincing that the reader forgets that it's all made up: others aim to remind the reader at every moment that fiction is not real life.

In this book, I haven't said much about the subject matter of writing. That's because I don't think it matters what the subject is, as long as the writing is alive. A small-scale, unassuming subject is just as worthy of fiction as a sweeping saga with profound philosophical underpinnings. Fiction is about what it's like to be human, so it can cover the entire range of our experiences.

Some writers know from the start what their subject is and have something they passionately want to say. Other writers discover their subject as they go along. If you have a feeling, no matter how vague, that you'd like to write something, that's enough to start with. As you write, you'll gradually discover what that feeling is about, and what your subject is.

Different kinds of fiction work for different readers. Some fiction is only appreciated by the person who wrote it: other fiction sells millions of copies. Some fiction is regarded as serious and is called 'literature', other fiction is regarded as ephemeral entertainment. These judgements differ because individuals differ, and also because cultures change: a book might be a best-seller in 1850 or 1950 and be completely unread today. Writers can't worry too much about any of this because we can't predict exactly what readers might want. We can only uncover as clearly we can what we would like to say, and work at expressing it in the most powerful way we can.

I hope that writers who use this book will be encouraged to write whatever shape and size of fiction they wish. I don't believe there's a correct way to write fiction. However, I also don't believe that any old writing will do. I believe that each writer has something to express, and that the art of writing is to discover the shape, size and colour of writing that is the most forceful way of bringing it to a reader.

There are two main ways through which this process will be illustrated:

1 Exercises in writing
Each chapter has several pages of exercises. These are designed to build on each other. The first exercise in each chapter is simple and straightforward. Once your first words are on the page, you will progressively modify what you've written as you proceed through the other exercises. By the end of this book, those first words will have become a piece of fiction: probably a short story, but you may find you have the material for a novel.

2 Examples of types of writing
The examples are drawn from contemporary Australian fiction and there is a great variety of styles and intentions. This ought to put to rest the idea that there's any 'right' way to write.

Who can use this book?

If you've already written a story and you know that it needs more work, this book will give you many new approaches to explore, as well as ways to open the story out in other directions and techniques for re-thinking and revising. If you're starting with a blank page, this book will take you progressively through all the steps in writing a story, from the first tentative words on the paper to a polished final version. In either case, each chapter in this book invites you to build on what went before so that a piece of writing gradually takes shape as you work through the book.

How to use this book

Chapter 1 demonstrates many different ways to overcome paralysis of the pen and get some words down on the paper. At the end of this chapter you'll have a pile of fragments.

Chapter 2 demonstrates how you can use these fragments as the raw material for further writing. You'll see how to sift through them, eliminating some, expanding others and grouping some together in order to see where you might go next. If you're just starting, at the end of this chapter you may have the embryo of a story. If you're working on an already written story, you'll have much more material which may suggest ways to re-think your work.

Chapters 3 to 8 are about ways to explore and refine this material. Each of these chapters focuses on a particular technical aspect of writing: point of view, dialogue, description and so on. If you're starting with nothing, at the end of Chapter 8 you'll have a substantial amount of writing which will be taking shape as a story. If you're working on an old story, you'll have systematically explored each aspect of its construction and will have plenty of new material and ideas.

Chapter 9 is about revising in order to focus more clearly or more vividly on the main thrust of the story. By the end of this chapter, you should have a complete piece of fiction.

Chapter 10 presents some guidelines for submitting your piece to a publisher.

Getting Started

I T doesn't matter where you start: the only thing that matters is where you finish. As Ezra Pound said, it doesn't matter which leg of your table you make first, as long as it stands up in the end.

Once you've got something on the page, you have something to work on. Anything that prevents you getting those first words on the page has to be avoided. High expectations and thinking about the finished product rather than the task at hand can have a paralysing effect on those first words.

There's a time to think about the story as a whole. There's a time to ask yourself what your story is about, or what it means. There's a time to demand the best of yourself. But the time to do those things is not at the beginning. At the beginning, the only thing that matters is to get some words, any words, on the paper.

Why is that so hard? Sometimes it's because our minds are blank but sometimes it's because our minds aren't blank enough. Sometimes our minds are full of voices, whispering advice to us about how to write. They drown out the voice of our own mind which, at this stage, needs all the encouragement it can get.

The whispering voices of advice

The whispering voices might say things like these:

'Just begin at the beginning.'
This sounds easy. The problem is that starting at the begin-

ning is just about the hardest place to start. The beginning of a piece of writing, as we all know, has to be irresistible. It has to grab the readers' attention and then glue them to the page. Great beginnings look easy but they don't come out of thin air; they come out of the whole story. Until the story is written, it's often hard to write a great beginning for it.

'First work out what you want to say.'
Many writers work this way. They work out their ideas, write down a plan and then just flesh it all out on the paper. However, many writers can't work this way because they don't quite know what they want to say until they've said it. Both ways of writing work, so if you can't work out what you want to say, don't let that hold you back. Once you've written something—and the exercises at the end of this chapter will take care of that—you'll have a better idea of what you want to say.

'First know your characters.'
Some writers do, but other writers get to know them as they go along. If you can't even think of any characters, let alone *know* them, you can still start to write.

'Writing should be grammatically correct.'
Most writing ends up being grammatically correct because it's easier for other people to read that way, but not all writing's like that. Look at the example on p. 69. In any case, when you first put pen to paper you're the only one reading it, so feel free to do what you like. You can fix up the grammar later.

'Writing has to have an interesting style.'
Some writing does, some writing doesn't. Look at the examples from Shirley Hazzard on pp. 5–6 and Gerald Murnane on pp. 6–7. They both make you want to find out what happened next, although only the Hazzard piece has a highly 'literary' style. You might decide that your finished story should be written in an elaborate style using similes and metaphors and so on, but, unless that style comes naturally, don't worry about it for your first draft. It can all be added later.

'Writing has to have a strong story.'
How interesting is it to have someone tell you the plot of a book they've just read? Not very. This means that plot alone isn't what makes a book interesting. What makes it interesting isn't *what's* told but *the way* it's told. In some of the best stories, almost nothing happens. See the example from Olga Masters, pp. 7–8.

'Write about what you know.'
This is good advice because writing seems to have more energy when it comes out of something the writer has experienced. However, it's not very helpful advice if you don't feel you know anything worth writing about. Some of the exercises at the end of the chapter invite you to write about what you know, but others invite you write in another way. When you do these exercises, you might find that you know something you didn't know you knew.

'If you can't write great literature it's not worth doing.'
'Literature' is a finished product. Once it's finished, it is hard to imagine it wasn't always as perfect as it is now. The literature we study by the great writers of the past is usually not their early work. Like the rest of us, they had to practise before they got it right, and when you look at their first drafts you realise that even they didn't always know what they were doing.

All that we now call 'literature' was once just writing, and all those writers we now call 'great' were once just people trying to write. If you want to learn to write well, you should read the work of those writers but it's discouraging to compare your own work with theirs too soon. One day, you too may write 'great literature' but if you try to write it from day one, you're more likely not to write at all.

'You have to be inspired.'
Few serious writers wait for inspiration to strike; they find it better to make regular work habits and stick to them, even if they're not in the mood. Some writers can work for eight or twelve hours at a stretch, others find that an hour or two is all they can usefully do. Some writers have unlimited time, some have the restrictions of other jobs, households to run, children to look after. Some writers use word processors,

some use typewriters, some use pens or pencils. Every writer works out a personal routine for working. Writing is one of the most individual things you'll ever do, so you'll gradually develop your own individual way of doing it. It doesn't matter how or when you write, as long as you keep doing it.

'You must write without distractions.'
If you live without distractions, this is good advice, but most of us are constantly distracted by other thoughts, worries, noises and sights. It may be impossible to eliminate distractions, but it's often possible to use them. Find a way to put the distraction, whatever it is, into your fiction, and write about it.

My only advice to writers is this: don't listen to the voices. Writers have to unlearn a lot before we are free to write. We have to unlearn a lot of the things we've learned, such as all the pieces of advice above. We have to unlearn, for a while, the desire to have a finished product. Getting a piece of writing to work usually means many failed attempts.

Hardest of all, we have to unlearn a lifetime's training in being orderly and making sense. Writers have to end up making sense but they don't have to start off making sense. In fact, a certain amount of apparent disorder is healthy in the early stages of writing. Why? Because being orderly is a process of eliminating things, and when you first start a piece of writing, it's better to have far more material than you need and more ideas than can possibly fit into the piece. You need to have a great untidy overflow of characters, events, images and moods so that you can pick and choose, rather than having a poor thin little heap.

This takes practice. At first, it may feel self-indulgent, pointless and messy. This is alarming. Remind yourself of two things: first, that this is only an early draft, not the finished product; and second, that you are the only person reading this.

And try not to ask the most paralysing question of all: 'but what is this all about?'

H ERE are some examples of openings to fiction that reach out and grab you and don't let you put the book down.

When we were thirteen, the coolest things to do were the things your parents wouldn't let you do. Things like have sex, smoke cigarettes, nick off from school, go to the drive-in, take drugs, and go to the beach.

- From *Puberty Blues*, Kathy Lette, p. 1.

Harry Joy was to die three times, but it was his first death which was to have the greatest effect on him, and it is this first death which we shall now witness.

- From *Bliss*, Peter Carey, p. 7.

Notice something about them, though. As well as being openings, they are also summaries, which means they might have been written last, not first.

The next two examples aren't so much summaries as statements of the theme: moods and images that set the context for the rest of the book.

By nightfall the headlines would be reporting devastation.

It was simply that the sky, on a shadeless day, suddenly lowered itself like an awning. Purple silence petrified the limbs of trees and stood crops upright in the fields like hair on end. Whatever there was of fresh white paint sprang out from downs or dunes, or lacerated a roadside with a streak of fencing. This occurred shortly after midday on a summer Monday in the south of England.

As late as the following morning, small paragraphs would even appear in newspapers having space to fill due to a hiatus in elections, fiendish crimes, and the Korean

War—unroofed houses and stripped orchards being given in numbers and acreage; with only lastly, briefly, the mention of a body where a bridge was swept away. That noon a man was walking slowly into a landscape under a branch of lightning. A frame of almost human expectancy defined this scene, which he entered from the left-hand corner. Every nerve—for even barns and wheelbarrows and things without tissue developed nerve in those moments—waited, fatalistic. Only he, kinetic, advanced against circumstances to a single des-tination.

> • From *Transit of Venus*, Shirley Hazzard, p. 3.

It was the afternoon of the thunderstorm when A. finally decided to fall in love with Nola Pomeroy or try to shag her or do something special with her in some out-of-the-way place.

The clouds began piling up late in the morning. Storms in summer usually came from the south west, where the ocean lay. But this one appeared from an unlikely quarter. A. watched it almost from its begin-nings through the north windows of the school. Its black bulk was bearing down on Sedgewick North from the plains far inland.

After lunch the sky over the school showed nothing but bulging clouds that tore away continually and drifted like smoke on turbulent currents. A. had just seen the first of the lightning when Mr Farrant told the seventh grade that their film strip on Major Mitchell was ready in the cloakroom and asked them what they were waiting for. They filed out through the door. Mr Farrant called after them: 'You, A., turn the projector and read the text and send the wrigglers and gigglers back to me.'

The cloakroom was so dark that A. could not see who had gone into the lovers' corner. But the darkness made the pictures more sharp and clear than any he had seen before. He showed the map of south-eastern Australia with a wide blankness over nearly all of Victoria. He went on turning the knob. Mitchell's dotted line left the Murray River and thrust southwards. A.'s audience was unusually quiet and solemn. He supposed they were

waiting for the first heavy drops of rain on the iron roof.
• From 'The Only Adam', Gerald Murnane, in *Faber Book of Contemporary Australian Short Stories*, p. 259.

Each of these examples starts with an attention-grabbing sentence, then moves away to focus on the weather before homing in on an individual character. In this way, a link can be established right in the beginning between large impersonal movements—represented by the weather—and individual lives. Notice how we're told some basic facts about where and when the story is set, but this rather dull though necessary information is embedded in much more dramatic material.

• • •

'It's today,' the fat child said and rolled over in bed landed on her feet on the floor and held the window sill, looking back at her sister, the thin one who had been jerked awake.
'Today!' the fat one said.
The thin one half raised herself on her elbows in bed. Her straight hair fell over her face. The fat one had curly hair in corkscrews over her head.
'Should be the other way round,' a visitor said once, looking at them with a stretched mouth and blank eyes.
The visitor meant that straight hair would have taken away from the fat one's rounded look and curls might have made the thin one look rounder.
The foster mother looked at them not bothering to stretch her mouth.
The fat one and the thin one looked away not knowing how to apologize for being the way they were.
'Go and play,' the foster mother said, but they were already going.
The fat one picked up a brush now and pressed it down her curls which sprang back in the wake of the bristles.
When she put the brush down she saw in the mirror her hair was the same as before.
The thin one screwed her body so that she could see

the fat one's reflection. 'Are you?' she said.

'Am I what?' the fat one answered.

'You know.' The thin one moved a foot which need not have belonged to her body so flat were the bedclothes. 'Excited about it,' the thin one said.

'Yes!' said the fat one, too loud and too sudden.

Tears came into the thin one's eyes. 'Don't shout!' she said.

The fat one picked up the brush and began to drag at her curls again. The thin one's watery eyes met her sister's in the mirror. They looked like portraits on a mantlepiece, the subjects photographed while the tension was still in their expression.

The foster mother came into the room then. She made the third portrait on the mantlepiece.

The thin one started to get out of bed rather quickly. Her ears were ready for the orders so she began to pull blankets off for the bedmaking.

But the foster mother said, 'Leave that.'

The thin one didn't know what to do then. She thrust a finger up her nose and screwed it round.

The foster mother covered her face with both hands. After a while she took them away showing a stretched mouth.

'Now!' she said quite brightly looking between them.

Now what? thought the fat one and the thin one.

Their mouths hung a little open.

The foster mother squeezed her eyes shut.

> • From 'The Home Girls', Olga Masters, in
> *The Home Girls*, pp. 1–2.

In the above story by Olga Masters, it's fairly obvious from the start that nothing earth-shattering is going to take place. But the way the humble domestic details are set in a context of irony makes you want to read on.

• • •

This is the legend of Wendy Trull who was the prettiest girl in Tasmania between 1955 and, say, 1959. A long time to hold any title, particularly that of beauty queen.

When you see a beginning like that, you know that Wendy must either triumph over terrible odds and end up as the wife of a diplomat, or she must be doomed. Will Wendy be found at the bottom of the cliff, broken like a wax doll, with strange juices oozing out, and her ears in a paper bag, you wonder; or will she have a wedding in the Cathedral, and an ironing lady, and a second house at the beach, perhaps even a third in the mountains and a flat in London? And for the children a nanny who is more like a second mother to them than a servant. What is going to happen to Wendy?

Wendy lived with her mother and father and brother and sisters in a reasonably nice house with wide verandahs on Windmill Hill. The needles from the pine trees collected on the verandahs, and one of Wendy's jobs was to sweep them up and put them in the incinerator. Wendy's granny lived in a grim old terrace house in a poorer part of the town. She kept the brass doorknob on the front door gleaming, and in the passage, just inside the door, she kept a cow. You opened the door, and there, standing sadly on the pink and green lino, was a brown and white cow. Cows' eyes look very big indeed when you see them up close in the narrow dimness of an entrance hall.

If there are motifs and links in the lives of people, then the presence of the cow in her granny's passage can be related to the presence of a secret lover in Wendy's attic. There were many years between the cow and the lover, but Buttercup, certainly an unusual pet, is somehow linked in Wendy's life to the man in the attic.

• From *Buttercup and Wendy*, Carmel Bird, pp. 49–50.

In the example above, there's a beginning that teases us with the kind of attention-grabbing first sentence that traditional fiction uses, but before we can relax into the reading trance, it is broken. This beginning promises that it's going to joke us along on two levels of meaning: one where we want to find out what happens to the characters and another where we're looking at the mechanism of the storytelling process itself. The everyday and the fantastic are put in the same frame so that there's leakage from one to the other: the beauty queen becomes strange and the cow in the hall becomes normal through this kind of two-layered vision.

It is not entirely an impersonal study of the process, though. Have a look at the way 'you' is used and imagine how much less intimate and engaging the piece would feel without it.

T HERE are three groups of exercises here, representing different techniques for getting started. Do some from each group because the aim at this point is to free your imagination and let it explore unknown paths. Think of these as nothing more than warm-up exercises and don't judge them as pieces of writing. The more you're surprised by what you find yourself writing, the better these exercises are working.

Group 1 Improvisations
Many writers use some kind of improvisation as a way to start. Improvisations are a way of tapping into the unconscious mind rather than the controlled conscious level. Improvisations can help you remember forgotten moments of the past and let you think thoughts that might have been censored or ridiculed into silence. Improvisations are likely to be your own ideas and your own natural language rather than second-hand thoughts and language borrowed from other books or TV.

In the course of writing an improvisation, you're likely to write about what you're really interested in and what you're really thinking about. This will help to answer the question: 'What should I write about?'

To get in the mood, start with a completely unstructured improvisation:

1.1 Write for 60 seconds without stopping. Just write exactly what comes into your head, even if it's only 'I can't think of anything to write this is a stupid thing to do.' Don't write in proper sentences or proper punctuation unless it comes out that way.

If you think you can't do this because there's not a single thought in your head, sit for 60 seconds with a completely blank mind. Not a single thought, not even about how hard the chair is or how much you'd like lunch. Is it possible?

Here's another kind of improvisation, one that gives you a starting point:

1.2 Self-Portrait: write about yourself as you are at this moment, using all five senses. What are you seeing? How does it look, how much of it can you see, what colours are there, what kind and quality of light is there? What are you hearing? Is it a constant noise, what causes it, what else might cause it? Is there another noise behind it that you only hear if you listen especially for it? Are any of these sounds like other sounds, do they remind you of anything else, do they make you feel a certain way? What are you touching, is it smooth, hard, cold? What else does it feel like? Do different parts of your body feel different things? Are you comfortable? What would make you more or less comfortable? How are you sitting or standing? What mood does this posture indicate? What are you smelling? Are you tasting anything? Can you imagine a taste? What would you like to be tasting? Can you describe that taste? If something distracts you from writing, write about this distraction.

Those improvisations were about the here-and-now but you can also improvise about the past. Which bit of the past? See what you start writing about when you do the following exercise:

1.3 Write the words 'I remember' at the top of a piece of paper and then see what comes out.

Write the words 'Yesterday, I' at the top of a piece of paper and see what you find yourself writing next.

Improvisations don't have to use your own experiences as a starting point. Words and objects can get you started just as well.

1.4 Write one of the following words and phrases at the
top of a page and then write for 60 seconds. Write
whatever comes into your head about the word: something it reminds you of, someone you think of when
you hear the word, an emotion it makes you feel.
Mushrooms. Gorgeous. Telephone. Shout. Fur. Never.
You wouldn't have thought... She wasn't a... Lying
face down...
Or take an object—either one you can see or one in
your mind—and do the same thing. The object might
be a stone, a leaf, a car, a photo, a painting, a garbage
bin or anything else.

Improvisation is all about hearing the voice of the unconscious, which we don't normally hear. One place we do
hear it, though, is in our dreams which, for that reason, are
often good starting points for writing.

1.5 Write about a dream you had recently, even if you can
only remember scraps of it. Now look at the scraps: do
any of them make you think of something else? Is there
anything in waking life that they make you think of?
What is the mood of the dream? Use the scraps as the
starting point for an improvisation.

Some people write down their dreams regularly, often as
part of a journal. This is a good idea for writers: a journal
can be a grab-bag of anything at all that you notice or think.
You can note down dreams and events from life and also
jokes you've heard, slips of the tongue, misprints, signs and
ads that you've noticed, things that you found interesting or
puzzling in books or films, descriptions of people or animals
or places, emotions you've felt and their causes, ideas
you've had. Your journal is just for you, so you can write it
in any way you like and anything at all can go into it. You
don't have to write in it every day, though the more you
start doing it, the more intriguing things you'll start notic-
ing. Once you have a journal, you can use a phrase or an

idea from it as the basis for an improvisation, and later on you can ransack it for settings, characters and so on.

There's a point where improvisation is almost exactly the same as the process of writing fiction. Here's an exercise where they come very close:

1.6 Without trying to think of a story, describe a character: male or female, their age, race, occupation, physical appearance and mood at this moment. Where is this character: city, country; inside, outside; rich, poor surroundings; cold, hot environment; alone or with others?

Now describe the same things about another character. The second character needn't have anything to do with the first. Then, connect these two characters. Do they already know each other? If they don't, is there a way in which they meet each other? If they already know each other, are they related by love, hate, accident or physical proximity? Is there a significant object which is important to the characters? Does one of the five senses predominate? What is the overall mood: menacing, domestic, meditative, etc?

Write a page in which these two characters interact.

If you're finding it hard to think of characters, start by improvising a setting and then add the characters later, like this:

1.7 Describe a place, a room or a landscape or some other kind of environment. What's the time of day, the weather, are we in the city or the country, are we inside or outside, is it hot or cold, is it a pleasant place or not, what can be heard, seen or smelled? Now some person enters this scene: furtively, violently, casually, accidently?

Group 2 Using someone else's story

This is a kind of improvisation, too, but you're improvising on a tune someone else has already written. That means you don't have to worry about structure: that's already there. You don't have to worry about plot: that's already there. You can concentrate on bringing your own voice to the story and focusing on what it is that you find interesting about it.

You might worry that if you're using other people's work or copying them, you'll never be able to write in your own way. Don't worry about that yet: if you're still copying another writer in your tenth draft, then worry. Try, though, to borrow from various writers, with different styles and voices, so that you don't get locked into one way of doing it.

1.8 Re-tell a story from somewhere: a newspaper story, a myth, a fairy-story, a joke, a story your mother told you.

Ask yourself, why have I chosen this particular story to use rather than another? Is it to do with the events? Or is it the people in it? Is it something I don't understand about the story that makes me want to re-tell it? Is it similar to something I've experienced myself? If it's sad, what exactly makes it sad? If it's funny, what exactly makes it funny? If it's sad, what would you have to do to it to make it funny? If it's funny, what would you have to do to make it tragic?

The answers to these questions might suggest another way of telling the story that is further from the original: more your own invention and less the story you've borrowed. Re-tell it again, making use of the answers to the above questions.

Sometimes it's not the plot of someone else's story that draws you to that piece of writing, but the actual words the writer's used or a mood that the original has created. It's often hard to say just how it has been done but you might be able to borrow a voice you like by doing this:

1.9 Choose a piece of writing you like. Use the first sentence as the opening for a piece you write yourself; or take the last sentence of the piece of writing and use it to conclude your piece. Another way is to look through the piece of writing until you come to a phrase or sentence that particularly takes your attention. Improvise a page of writing, using this phrase or sentence in any way you like.

There is some magic about the rhythm of sentences, the way the words are put together, that can make a piece of writing very powerful and musical. There's no reason why you shouldn't borrow some of that magic.

1.10 Take a couple of sentences that you like from another story. Now, leaving the structure of each sentence exactly the same, replace the words with words of your own.

Here's an exercise for those who relish chaos:

1.11 Take a few pages of some writing that you like. Cut the pages up into phrases or words, put all the bits into a box and then pull them out and stick them together at random. You'll have a lot of nonsense and you'll also have a few suggestive, odd connections: ways of putting words together that you'd never have thought of otherwise. Take some of these connections and use them as the basis for an improvisation.

This next exercise doesn't just borrow from someone else's story but from someone else's life.

1.12 Eavesdrop on a conversation: on a bus, at a party, in the street, or even one end of a phone conversation. Write down what you can remember of it, then use it as the basis for a page of writing. Ask these sorts of questions to get going: what are these characters like? What sort of life histories do they have? Do they like each other, fear each other, despise each other, are they about to fall in love? What are they doing while they talk? Where are they? What are they about to do next?

Group 3 Word games
These exercises are at the other end of the spectrum from the first ones which were improvisations based on yourself. These ones take as their starting point something quite impersonal: games with words.

No one expects great literature or anything very profound to come out of word games so they're a good way of writing in an unself-conscious way. Word games are an excellent way of jerking the mind out of its usual groove. In these exercises, the rules of the game force you to put words together and create meanings in ways you may never think of otherwise. Sometimes there's no meaning and that's useful, too, because it's a reminder that words are just artificial games themselves which only mean something because we've all agreed that they should.

Some of these might sound silly. But try them: you might be surprised at what you find yourself writing.

1.13
- Write a paragraph without using the letter 'e'.
- Write a paragraph in which the first word starts with 'a', the second word starts with 'b' and so on through the alphabet.
- Go through the dictionary and collect ten words that catch your eye. Write a piece that will use them all.
- Take a sentence at least ten words long, from any-where. Then use each word in the sentence as the first word of a new sentence.

All these improvisations are just starting points. It's unlikely that any of them will appear in their present form in your finished work. But, whereas before you had a blank page, you now have quite a few pieces of writing. They may seem to you to have no value and not to lead anywhere but they are the raw material out of which a piece of writing may take shape. In the next chapter, we'll sift through them and begin the process of turning them into a story.

2. Sorting Through

A T this point, you have a few pages of writing. There are bits and pieces of dreams, memories, improvisations and word games. The next stage is the beginning of making a story out of this random—or seemingly random—collection.

Making piles

The first step in shaping a story is to sort through your collection of raw material. Have a look at all the pieces you have and see if you can sort them into different piles—categories of one kind or another.

What you're looking for are elements that go together or connect in some way. They don't have to connect in any logical way; the connection can be nothing more than an intuition that a couple of things are related. At this stage, your material doesn't have to add up to anything, or be a story.

The most basic kinds of categories you might begin with are 'good bits' and 'boring bits'. You might have a pile for all the bits you've written that are trying to be funny, and another pile for the serious ones. You could have a pile for the pieces that are about the same person. You might find that you've mentioned the same word in more than one of your pieces, and so you could put those pieces together.

You might have a pile called 'events' and one called 'ideas' or 'generalisations'. There might be a 'real life' pile and an 'imaginary' pile. There might be a 'present tense' pile and a 'past tense' pile. Any kind of connection will be enough to start with.

The advantages of piles

The advantage of working this way is that you are using material you already have and letting it direct you. This is easier, and more likely to open up further ideas, than starting off with an idea that you then have to force material to fit.

In all those improvisations, you were free to write about anything at all. That means that what you ended up writing about was probably something that matters to you. What it is, and why it matters, is still buried deeply in those pieces but the process of looking for connections is the first step in uncovering it.

The fragments mightn't seem to relate to each other at all, at first glance, but they already have several things in common. Firstly, they were all written by the same person — they all came out of your mind, and your mind alone. Secondly, they were probably written within a fairly short space of time so it's likely that similar ideas or moods will be in several of them.

Ways of making piles

If you only have a few piles, you can keep track of them in your head. Alternatively, you could use markers of different colours to mark different categories, write lists on another piece of paper or make notes in the margin.

Sometimes you can see connections more clearly if you physically move the pieces of writing around. You can cut up your pages of writing so that you can separate out all the different categories as you start to see them. Make a photo-copy first in case you want to go back to the original. Then you can move them around and see how different bits read together. Screen writers often write a summary of their scenes onto different index cards and then lay them out and re-arrange them on the floor.

To demonstrate the process, I'll show you the pieces I wrote in response to the exercises in Chapter 1 and what sort of piles I'd make out of those pieces.

First, I improvised for 60 seconds and wrote this:

> I am going to write for 60 seconds, what am I going to write about, I can't think of anything at all to write about my mind is a complete blank. I'm sitting at the desk. Mainly I'm conscious of being cold around the edges. My feet are cold and my shoulders are feeling a draught from the door, which is open so I can hear if Tom wakes up from his nap. I had a cup of coffee a few minutes ago to warm myself up and I can still taste that old-penny taste of instant coffee in my mouth. Outside, next door they're laying the concrete slab for the house that's going up next door. Actually just now they're shovelling the earth into very level square mounds and then laying huge squares of plastic on it — sort of giant glad-bags. I can hear the scrape of the shovels, they're working very slowly, when you just listen you realise how slowly they're working although when you're watching them you'd think they were going quite fast. But there are long pauses between the shovel noises. Outside it's a sunny morning and I've just noticed that the plane-tree down the road has lost its leaves since I last looked. Winter is in the air. Hearing those shovels next door, like grave-digging shovels slowly shaping the earth, and thinking about winter coming makes me feel anxious and a bit gloomy.

Then I happened to hear a piece of music on the radio called *The Moldau* — I remembered hearing this at school and wrote an improvisation on what the music made me remember.

> 'I remember listening to *The Moldau* in the hot little portable class-room where we learned music. I don't

remember the music at all but I remember what the teacher said about it: she said this was the national song of Hungary, no it was some particular group of Hungarians it was. They were a distinct group and had once been a nation but were now part of the country of Hungary. This song was their national song and since they were now supposed to be part of Hungary they were forbidden to sing it. Or was it that they were invaded by Germany in WWII and forbidden to sing it then? In any case they did sing it, as a sign of resistance, and people were shot for singing this forbidden song. I remember finding that very frightening. What if you just started to hum it in an absent-minded way. Would you still be shot. I remember that I'd just got into deep trouble for whistling in the corridor between lessons without really realising I was doing it. I'd had a long lecture from Miss Rush about it.

Next I did a couple of the word games, first writing a paragraph without using the letter 'e'.

If anything was utilitarian, it was glass. Smashing satisfyingly on floors, lifting full of fluid, no pocks or pits, smooth as a baby's bottom and anonymous. Folk lifting glass to lips and drinking: souls smoothing out. For brains, what is in glass is good, for all swims smoothly with a lifting of an arm on two or possibly four occasions. No worry then, just much chat. Chat do much to simplify a man's mind. Chat fills up gaps in a man's soul. Chat, sawdust, a glass at lip and glass on walls up to waist—not so dirty that way—swill down all walls at closing and throw out all drunks. I fancy a glass or two if took with a good man or two: a bar is a boy's good companion.

This had the interesting effect of forcing a kind of foreign accent or pidgin quality into the writing, and I was surprised to find myself writing about an old-style pub, and writing from the point of view of someone very different from myself.

I was sent a postcard of a painting—Geoffrey Smart's

painting, *Cahill Expressway*. This is very realistic and rather threatening; it shows the tunnel of the Cahill Expressway, with a monument and some stone buildings in the background. In the foreground, a man in a blue suit stands and looks at the viewer. I improvised on the painting and came up with these notes:

> We've built a tunnel and lined it with shiny tiles and covered every inch of dirt with tons of concrete and asphalt, what was it before, part of the Botanical Gardens, before that bush, perhaps the Aborigines gathered there, it would have been a good spot by the Harbour, plenty of food, interesting to take one square yard of the surface of the earth and write the history of everything that's ever happened on that spot from the beginning of time. The Expressway is one of the approaches to the Harbour Bridge, the opposite, not a tunnel but an arch, but another monument, another marvel of technology.
>
> The tunnel is light into dark, leaving the light behind, a moral symbol. But the decision to build public monuments not always a moral one. Political convenience or a payoff, or the lure of technology, once you invent reinforced concrete you have to find something to build with it.
>
> Some decisions are irrevocable: impossible to ever demolish, to restore that bit of earth to its natural state. How do we arrive at those decisions, who exactly decides to build an expressway or a tunnel or a monument. The Ozymandias syndrome, money waiting to be spent, prestige, beat other cities. Other monuments of antiquity, all in ruins now, tourists of the future will come & look at the ruins of our tunnels & bridges. Like the Pyramids, Roman viaducts, Great Wall of China. Is the man in the blue suit Ozymandias looking on his works with pride, or is he the engineer or the politician who's created it?
>
> The monument in the background — to World War I? Is the man in the suit a fat businessman making money out of fine sentiments?
>
> There is a tidy sum to be made out of a statue, if a man has his head screwed on. And there is no shame in being the middleman. Even Tutankhamun must have

had sub-contractors and at the end of the day they must have made a packet.

The Cahill Expressway postcard had made me think about the Pyramids, and that in turn had made me remember a poem I'd learned at school, *Ozymandias*, by Shelley. The poem is about a king who had a huge statue of himself made. The poem points out his vanity in thinking it would stand for ever; it's now in ruins. I took the first line of the poem, which was all I could remember of it, and wrote from that, starting again several times when I ran out of steam.

I met a traveller from an antique land. I'm quoting his words, of course, I myself would never be so vague. I met a traveller, in some pub or other. I travel, he said. In nuts, bolts and statuary. It happened that I didn't need any nuts or bolts. But a nice bit of statuary never goes amiss.
I am a traveller, he said. From an antique land.
Where, exactly, I asked, for he was a swarthy shifty thick-tongued sort of fellow, making patterns in the sawdust with his shoe. Oh, he cried so that men near us turned, beers in hand, to stare. Oh! There is no use telling you, my friend, you will not have heard its name, now it is no more! He tossed back his beer as if it were some clear fiery liquor, stared at me for a moment during which I wondered if he might fling the glass to the floor. I began to wish I had not spoken to this gent who, I now observed, was as likely to be simply another reffo ratbag with a chip on his shoulder and garlic on his breath, as anything else.
I wished now to change the subject and quell the exclamations that he was starting to grow fond of. But I could see he was a reffo ratbag who liked an audience. And what is your business, here in Australia, I asked, making the word Australia sound as unromantic, as unantique, as prosaic and brick-and-tile as I could.
The reffo ratbag looked gloomy. Oh, he said with a sniff and a wipe of his nose with the back of his hand. I am a tiler. I tile walls, floor, anything, I could tile this glass if I wanted.
He came closer, so I could smell garlic and another,

dead smell like earth. I know a thing or two, mate, he said. I could tell you a thing or two, if I wished.

Then I took the word 'mushroom' and improvised:

Mushrooms grow in the dark from spores. Dad tried to grow mushrooms under the house once, he got a whole truck-load of straw and manure and bought the spores, I remember him spending a lot of time under there making little square raised mounds of dirt for the straw and manure to sit on, and swearing because it wasn't quite high enough for him to stand so he kept hitting his head on the beams. He went to a lot of trouble. This will make our fortunes, he'd say, this is going to make us rich. He poked and prodded and watered and hovered over those mounds of straw and he and Mum kept reminding themselves how it takes mushroom spores a very long time to germinate, I'd go down there some-times and find him just standing staring at the mounds and he kept reading books about mushrooms but they never did sprout.

Then I wrote down a dream:

When I was little I had a recurring dream that I used to dread. In it I would be standing up on a stage, playing the violin. I was doing well; down in the front row I could dimly see the audience clapping and cheering. But then with a feeling of horror I would see that the stage I was standing on was being eaten away from all sides, rapidly getting smaller and smaller. No one else seemed to notice. I played faster and faster but I felt a great wave of panic. I kept wondering why no one noticed, why no one was doing anything to help me.

Next I tried the alphabet exercise, doing it twice to get a longer run at it:

Anyone being cautious doesn't enter foolishly, going hurriedly into jams. Knives like men numb, operating piercingly, quietly. Rather scared to undo voluntary wishes. Xenophobes yell 'Zero!'. A bricklayer came dancing, entwining fronds gaily. He inched jarringly, kindly leaving many neurones overjoyed. Particularly quaint, rabid stirring tunes undid vaults. Why, Xerxes, you zebra-striped?

Next I tried the sentence exercise. My original sentence was: 'After leaving her husband, she never could sleep in a double bed again.' I used each word in that sentence as the first word of a new sentence. This is what I ended up with:

After all, she thought, pets are a nuisance. Leaving fur everywhere, they create a constant mess. Her Manx cat—actually, it was his—for example moulted constantly. Husband! She thought. Never again will I look after your animals. Could you not have thought just a little about me, and not just gone off without even a note on the mantlepiece? Sleep, that was all she wanted to do now, sleep in a narrow bed with cool edges. In fact what about a hammock? A hammock is like a womb, like a chaste embrace, like swinging through the trees again, comforting and full of forgetfulness. Double hammocks have probably been invented by some obsessed male or other, she thought. Bed, hammock, couch, chaiselongue—they came to them all with one thing on their minds. Again and again and again, until a body was weary of them.

I now had seven pages of these fragments and went through them looking for connections. Someone else might have made different connections, but these are the ones I made.
1 Things to do with digging, earth, coldness, operating knives: gloomy death-associations.
2 Things to do with building: the house next door, the expressway, the monument, the tiler, the bricklayer.
3 Several characters:
   an 'I' who is myself, hearing the builders next door, having the dream, etc;
   an 'I', not myself, in the pub with the traveller and

25

again in a pub thinking about glass;
an 'I', not myself, who is a woman whose husband has just left;
an 'I' who speaks a kind of pidgin English.
4   Several styles:
a chatty naturalistic style — the first improvisation sitting at the desk, and the last about the mushrooms, among others;
a more formal style — the 'I' of 'I met a traveller . . .' and also the childhood dream;
the foreign style of the 'without e' exercise.

And I made another category for things that didn't seem to go anywhere: 'The Moldau' piece and most of the 'alphabet' exercises about zebras and Xerxes.

Musing on this some more, I felt that I could begin to glimpse a theme emerging. The first two categories were actually part of the one theme: how we proudly build our monuments — tunnels, statues, houses — and think they'll last, but at some point in the future even our best constructions will be ruins. A theme about Life and Death.

This was a theme which the chatty informal style didn't seem to suit. So I decided that the formal tone of the scene in the pub would be the one I'd go with, for the moment.

That brought me to the question of the characters: who is the 'I' who meets the traveller from an antique land? Is it the women whose husband has just left, leaving the Manx cat behind? Is she drinking too much out of loneliness and striking up conversations with anyone? This didn't seem right because the formal tone of 'I met a traveller. . .' didn't seem to be in tune with the person she seemed to be. So I put her to one side for the time being.

I looked at the postcard again and wondered if the man in the blue suit in the painting could be the 'I' who meets the traveller. What that left me with was something that felt like a beginning: man in blue suit goes into pub and starts talking to another man, who introduces himself as a traveller and a tiler. Since he's a traveller, perhaps he could be the speaker of the peculiar English — perhaps he's a foreigner as well as a traveller. The tiler is proud and confident about building things. The man in the blue suit is thinking gloomy thoughts about the temporary nature of all things.

Who is the man in the blue suit, and why is he thinking

gloomy thoughts? Has he just left his wife and his Manx cat? Or perhaps he is contemplating suicide for some reason or other. Or perhaps he is dying. If he was dying, I could use all the bits about the shovels sounding like grave-diggers. If he was dying, the image of operating kives cutting into flesh might be used.

Who is the 'traveller'? He is a foreigner with quirky English. His 'antique land' could be one of those countries of Europe that no longer exists: *The Moldau* piece could go back in, after all. Perhaps, when he's had his glass or four, the traveller sings his forbidden national song to the man in the blue suit.

Who is the woman who thinks about Manx cats and hammocks? I was reluctant to lose her altogether. Perhaps she is the wife of the man in the blue suit, or perhaps she's the barmaid.

Remembering the first line of *Ozymandias* triggered the improvisation that I found most interesting: the one in the pub. So I found a copy of the poem and looked at it.

Ozymandias

I met a traveller from an antique land
Who said: Two vast and trunkless legs of stone
Stand in the desert . . . Near them, on the sand,
Half sunk, a shattered visage lies, whose frown,
And wrinkled lip, and sneer of cold command,
Tell that its sculptor well those passions read
Which yet survive, stamped on these lifeless things,
The hand that mocked them, and the heart that fed:
And on the pedestal these words appear:
'My name is Ozymandias, king of kings:
Look on my works, ye Mighty, and despair!'
Nothing beside remains. Round the decay
Of that colossal wreck, boundless and bare
The lone and level sands stretch far away.
• P. B. Shelley

This poem is full of phrases that appealed to me and that seemed to suit my man in the blue suit. The old-fashioned language and stately rhythms seemed right for him. So I put

27

together a loose skeleton of a story, full of gaps and uncertainties, which consisted of pieces I'd written, phrases from the poem, and rough notes. It's still in piles, but the piles are starting to connect in a tentative way. At this point I'm concerned with arranging the piles rather than re-writing their content.

Pile 1: the opening

> I met a traveller from an antique land. I'm quoting his words, of course, I myself would never be so vague.
> I met a traveller, in some pub or other. 'I travel', he said, 'in nuts, bolts and statuary'. It happened that I didn't need any nuts or bolts. But a nice bit of statuary never goes amiss.
> 'I am a traveller', he said, 'from an antique land'.
> 'Where, exactly?' I asked, for he was a swarthy shifty thick-tongued sort of fellow, making patterns in the sawdust with his shoe. 'Oh', he cried so that men near us turned, beers in hand, to stare. 'Oh! There is no use telling you, my friend, you will not have heard its name, now it is no more! He tossed back his beer as if it were some clear fiery liquor, stared at me for a moment during which I wondered if he might fling the glass to the floor. I began to wish I had not spoken to this gent, who, I now observed, was as likely to be simply another reffo ratbag with a chip on his shoulder and garlic on his breath, as anything else.
> I wished now to change the subject and quell the exclamations that he was starting to grow fond of. But I could see he was a reffo ratbag who liked an audience. 'And what is your business, here in Australia?,' I asked, making the word Australia sound as unromantic, as unantique, as prosaic and brick-and-tile as I could.
> The reffo ratbag looked gloomy. 'Oh', he said with a sniff and a wipe of his nose with the back of his hand, 'I am a tiler. I tile walls, floor, anything, I could tile this glass if I wanted.'
> He came closer, so I could smell garlic and another, dead smell like earth. 'I know a thing or two, mate', he said. 'I could tell you a thing or two, if I wished.'

The other 'pub material' should go here:

If anything was utilitarian, it was glass. Smashing satisfyingly on floors, lifting full of fluid, unpocked and unpitted, smooth as a baby's bottom and anonymous. Folk lifting glass to lips and drinking: souls smoothing out. For brains, what is in glass is good, for all swims smoothly with a lifting of an arm on two or possibly four occasions. No worry then, just much chat. Chat do much to simplify a man's mind. Chat fills up gaps in a man's soul. Chat, sawdust, a glass at lip and glass on walls up to waist — not so dirty that way — swill down all walls at closing and throw out all drunks. I fancy a glass or two when took with a good man or two: a bar is a boy's good companion.

Pile 2: tells something about corruption in high places

The tunnel is light into dark, leaving the light behind, a moral symbol. But the decision to build public monuments not always a moral one. Political convenience or graft, or the lure of technology... how do we arrive at those decisions?

There is a tidy sum to be made out of a statue, if a man has his head screwed on. And there is no shame in being the middleman. Tutankhamun must have had sub-contractors and at the end of the day they must have made a packet.

Pile 3: man in blue suit thinks gloomy thoughts about mortality.

That makes me feel anxious and gloomy...

This will make our fortunes, this is going to make us rich... they never did sprout.

We've built a tunnel and lined it with shiny tiles and covered every inch of dirt with tons of concrete and asphalt.

Impossible to ever demolish, to restore that bit of earth to its natural state.

Other monuments of antiquity, all in ruins now, tourists of the future will come and look at the ruins of our tunnels & bridges. Like the pyramids, Roman viaducts, Great Wall of China.

Pile 4: phrases and images from *Ozymandias* that appeal

Vast . . . legs of stone . . . desert and sand . . . a stone head, half-sunk in the earth . . . sneer . . . Look on my works . . . decay . . . colossal . . . lone and level sands.

Pile 5: *The Moldau*

Perhaps the traveller sings his national song to the man in the blue suit. He would be embarrassed. Also might rather envy him for it.

This song was their national song and since they were now supposed to be part of Hungary they were forbidden to sing it . . . in any case they did sing it, and people were shot for singing this forbidden song.

Pile 6: the song makes the man in the suit think of his own life

Man in suit thinks how the song will live on after the singer is dead.

Man in blue suit thinks about what he himself has to leave behind after his death.

Thinks about his wife, who will then be a woman without a husband.

Couldn't you have thought just a little about me . . . A hammock is like a womb, like a chaste embrace . . . full of forgetfulness.

What is his relationship with his wife? Re-think this from his point of view: does he think about her much?

Pile 7: thinks about his own death

Thinks about the doctor who has just told him he's dying. Thinks about operations:

Anyone being cautious doesn't enter foolishly, going hurriedly into jams. Knives like men numb, operating piercingly, quietly. Rather scared to undo voluntary wishes.

Feels frightened:

I'm conscious of being cold around the edges. My feet are cold and my shoulders are feeling a draught from the door.

They're shovelling the earth into very level square mounds. I can hear the scrape of the shovels, they're working very slowly, there are long pauses between the shovel-noises.

Hearing those shovels next door, like grave-digging shovels slowly shaping the earth...

With a feeling of horror I see that the stage I was standing on was being eaten away... no one else seemed to notice... I felt a great wave of panic... why was no one doing anything to help me.

Chapter 9 shows the finished story that emerged from this rather unpromising start.

N ow you can try the 'piles' technique with your own material. Your own material might just be all the pieces you wrote for Chapter 1. You may also have other writing you've done, fragments or perhaps even complete stories, or you may have been writing a journal. Make a photocopy of any of this material so you're free to cut it up and scribble on it. Complete stories are the hardest to use because it's difficult to come freshly to them: be ruthless about cutting into their structure to extract, perhaps, just one sentence that you like.

You may find that there are very clear piles in what you've written, but if there aren't, try to find some by asking the following questions.

Questions about boredom

2.1 • Which bits do I like most, or dislike least?
  • What is the most interesting—or the least boring—thing about these pieces?
  • What is there in it that I don't understand, or don't know why I wrote it, or would like to write more about?
  • Which bits surprised me as I wrote them?
  • Are there any bits that are funny, deliberately or not?

These are especially good questions to apply to a complete story, because they give you a way to separate the story out into its parts again so you can re-assemble it differently.

So there you have one pile: 'good bits'.

Questions about themes

2.2 • Is there a word or image that I've used more than once?
  • Is there anything that sparks off a memory or makes me think of something else?

- Do some of the pieces have a similar mood? For example, humorous, nostalgic, sinister.

Questions about plot, or story line

2.3
- What happened next?
- What happened before that?
- Could any of the pieces be arranged so that they formed a sequence?
- Do any of the pieces feel like a beginning, or an end?

Questions about characters

2.4
- How many different characters have I got?
- Might any of them be combined to be all part of the one character?
- Could I arrange the characters in piles, from the one I've written most about, down to the one I've written least about?
- Are they all me, speaking in my own voice?
- What do I feel about them? Which one do I like most, and least?
- Could any of the characters connect — could they meet each other, or do they already know each other?

Can you separate your pieces out into piles of different writing styles?

2.5
- Do all the pieces sound the same, or do some sound different? For example, the word-game pieces are likely to sound different from the improvisations.
- Can I sort them into piles like slangy/formal, or my voice/another voice?

Questions about the structure of what you have.

2.6
- Is there one story here, or are there several quite separate ones?
- Is there some device I could use to connect all these pieces; for example, are they all things that one central character is finding out?
- Are they all things the one central character is doing?

- Are they all memories which could be threaded in and out of some present-time story?
- If they were all related from the same point of view, would they form a unit?

Then there are the pieces that don't seem to connect in any way at all. Put them in a separate pile, but don't throw them away because later on you might find them useful, after all.

Now try to string some of the piles together into some vague order. You can leave big gaps and sketch in rough notes to indicate what you might write later. Don't worry if your stringing together doesn't look anything like a story. You don't need a proper plot or characters: all you need at this stage is the flimsiest of skeletons. If you really don't have enough material to do this, go back to Chapter 1 and write some more fragments.

This skeleton is the basis for the next eight chapters. By the time you've worked through them, your skeleton will have plenty of flesh on it. Then you can decide if you like it. Don't give up on it yet!

3 Character

Now that you have a framework for your story, it's time to start filling it in. The next six chapters all focus on different ways to go about that: including characters, point of view, voice, dialogue, description and design. It's artificial, of course, to separate fiction out into its component parts and pretend that 'characters', for example, can be looked at separately from 'dialogue'. In finished fiction, nothing can be separated out like that. But until the fiction is finished, it can be a useful exercise to focus on one aspect at a time: otherwise the task can seem confusing and daunting.

In this chapter, we'll look at the idea of characters, because characters are usually the key to a piece of writing and they're often the simplest place to start. But that may not be true of the framework you've got. If one of the other chapters seems like a better place for you to start, do so.

What are characters?

One important thing about characters is that they're not the same as people. People are in life: characters are in fiction. Think of the expression 'he's a real character': what do we mean?

Characters in fiction come in many varieties. Frequently, they are very 'life-like' and when you read about them you feel you know them in the same way you know a person in life. Look at the example by Tim Winton on pp. 41–42. Other kinds of fiction aren't interested in creating convincing copies of real people: they deliberately aim for stylised, artificial characters so that you never forget that you're reading a piece of fiction rather than experiencing a piece of life. This has its own fascination: look at the examples by Carmel Bird on p. 8–9, and Richard Lunn on pp. 43–44.

As the writer, you might want the reader to be very sympathetic to a particular character or you might want the reader to loathe the character. Characters might be the whole point of a piece of fiction: it may be that nothing much happens and nothing very dramatic is said, but the characters are so interesting that that's enough. The extract from David Malouf on pp. 40–41 falls into this category. On the other hand, the characters might be a minor detail in a piece of writing that's really about a landscape, or an idea.

Characters can be surprising, so that the reader is kept guessing what they're going to do next. They can be completely predictable, so the reader can guess exactly what they're likely to do.

Writers make a choice, then, about what sort of characters they want and what function these characters will perform in the piece of fiction. Having made those choices, how do you make your characters do what you want?

Characterisation

Personally, I resist the idea of 'characterisation' as if it's something that you can smear on a bit of writing and produce characters. Characters are not people, but they are like people in being, finally, mysterious. Their delicate mechanisms can't be summed up neatly in formulas or rules.

Characterisation is all the things writers do to build up the characters they want. Characterisation is the process that transforms real-life people into characters in fiction.

On the subject of characters, those voices from Chapter 1 may be heard again. They may be saying things like these:

'Characters should be drawn from life'
As a writer, you're in the luxurious position of being able to

take from life whatever you want, but to ignore life if you want to. You may find that a real person makes a good basis for a character but you only have to use the parts of that person that you want to. You can make up the rest, or combine elements from several real people to make one character.

Characters that are drawn too closely and literally from life run the risk of not working as fiction, for several reasons:
- writers drawing on a person they know are likely to assume a lot about them and forget to tell the reader;
- real life and real people are sometimes stranger and more interesting than fiction, but one of the reasons we read books is that life is often a lot *less* interesting than fiction.

Even if a person is fascinating in life, simply transferring them to fiction is no guarantee that they'll be interesting on the page. Things that we accept in real life we don't necessarily accept in fiction. It's not enough just to draw a portrait of an odd person from life and say 'but they're really like that'. Life can get away with it: fiction can't.

So it's not enough for characters to be drawn from life for them to work as fiction. But on the other hand, if nothing about them is drawn from life, other problems can arise.
- It's very hard to produce an interesting character completely out of your own imagination. The danger here is that the character becomes a lifeless mouthpiece for the writer's ideas.
- A writer might, perhaps unconsciously, be using second-hand characters — not using people from real life as a basis, but characters from other books or TV. These characters have already been pruned and shaped to fit the context of their original story and if you transfer them to yours they will be very thin and shadowy.

'Characters shouldn't be allowed to take over from the writer.'
Writers disagree about this. Some writers need to be in complete control of their characters at all times, while others feel that their best characters 'come to them' fully formed and almost 'write themselves'. My feeling is that both approaches work, but at different times in the writing process.

Characters can be allowed to take over in early drafts. Usually this results in writing that's energetic and that flows out easily: characters can often 'write about themselves' for pages on end. However, in the end, the writer is boss and although it may feel as if the characters are writing themselves, it's the writer who's doing it all. The only difference is that when the character takes over, the writer is listening to the unconscious rather than the conscious mind.

The writer has to be able to recognise if a character has gone off in a direction that goes against the grain of the rest of the story, or is unbalancing the story by dominating it. The writer is the one who can decide, in later drafts, what it is that the story is trying to do, and then make sure that everything in the story, including characterisation, is shaped and controlled towards that aim.

'Characters must be consistent.'
Consistent characters run the risk of being boring characters. People aren't consistent and characters don't have to be either. Inconsistencies can make characters interesting, as long as they're inconsistent in a way that adds something to the story.

While perfectly consistent characters may be boring, perfectly inconsistent ones may be frustrating to a reader: they never add up to a coherent personality. Inconsistencies can add depth to a character, but they have to be carefully controlled by the writer.

'Characters should be thoroughly described and explained.'
Getting to know a character is similar to getting to know a person: the pleasure is in gradually finding things out and piecing them together for yourself. Sometimes in fiction, the writer will give a detailed description and explanation of the character. See for example Malouf on pp. 40–41. However, sometimes it can be more intriguing to a reader to have to work it all out for themselves. See for example Dickins, pp. 84–85.

'Characters must be lifelike.'
What does it mean to be 'lifelike'? Life is like so many different things.

Characters do have to be convincing, which is a different thing. Characters can be unlike anyone we have ever met and yet we can believe in them within the pages of the story. Characters in fiction don't have to work as people: they only have to work as characters in fiction. See p. 44–45 for an example of an 'unlifelike' character who works wonderfully as a piece of fiction.

'Characters must be interesting.'
There's no such thing as an interesting character, only interesting writing. The woman described by Tim Winton (pp. 41–42) mightn't be thought of as interesting in life but she becomes so through the writing.

'Characters have to be motivated.'
In real life, people are motivated by many different things and it's often not possible to point to a simple motive. Life is not a simple matter of cause and effect, and fiction doesn't have to be either.

As a writer, you don't have to explain or even know exactly what's making your characters do what they do: your only obligation is to make their actions convincing to the reader. That's easier said than done, and it relies on your instinct or intuition about people. Once you move away from the kind of fiction where every action has a simple motive behind it, you move into a subjective area where some readers will be convinced and others will not. This is why fiction is not a science, and it's also what makes it endlessly fascinating both to write and to read.

It's no good writing something you're feeling bored with, which may happen if characters are too neatly motivated, and too one-dimensional. You have to trust your instinct, and boredom is a great way to detect writing that is never going to work. The feeling that a piece of writing is coming too slowly can be another clue. Writing isn't usually easy but it shouldn't be like extracting teeth, either. If it's that hard, something's gone wrong. Stop what you're doing and go back to improvising until you get interested again. Writing should not become a kind of chore. If the writer is bored, the reader will be bored.

L IKE most sons I suppose, I had forced upon
my father the character that fitted most easily with
my image of myself; to have had to admit to any complexity in him would have compromised my own. I
chose the facts about him that I needed: his one solid
gold tooth that glowed when he laughed like a miracu-
lous image in a southern monastery; his habit of crossing himself whenever he passed a church; his talent for
walking on his hands along the beach at Scarborough,
strutting about like some exotic bird, carrying his body
through the air as if it were plumage, heavy, extraordinary. I found these images of him comfortingly foreign.
Like his skill at athletics (which I decided early I should
never try to equal) and his passion for building things.
Wearing a leather apron and shorts, with his tool box
open on the bench behind him, all its bits and chisels
neatly stacked, and a stub of pencil behind his ear, he
would work for long hours in the gloom under the
house, planing, sawing, working away with his chisel
and mallet at elegant dovetails and grooves. He built us,
at one time or another, a caravan, two beach houses
with beds that went up into the wall, several monstrous
wall units, box-kites, a model sailing boat, a set of
swings, and before we abandoned the old house re-
placed all its cast-iron and venetians with fibro and
glass. He had left school at eleven to become a post-boy
on the Nanango mails and had never, so far as I knew,
read a book. All of this was a gap between us and left
my notion of my own independence utterly uncom-
promised. Now suddenly I was not so sure.

Everywhere here there was evidence of a life I had
failed to take account of—birthday cards he had sent
my mother during their twelve-year courtship (huge
boxlike affairs, all padded velvet and handpainted cellu-
loid), letters, sketches, even an old leather diary of 1928
in which he had jotted down, over the years, some of
the 'facts' that struck him: the population of Madrid in
1957 (the year he and my mother went to Europe), a list

of all the paintings and items of furniture in Room 4 of the Wallace Collection, and the dimensions of various rooms he had modernized (provided, that is, with one of his built-in units) when he was buying and selling houses in the suburbs.

• From *Johnno*, David Malouf, pp. 5–6.

In this extract, David Malouf is building up two characters, the father and the son. The son is telling the story: he has power over which details he will remember and draw our attention to. He has the same power the writer has. However, in the second paragraph he reminds us how the selection of different details can build up quite a different character altogether. Both in choosing certain details rather than others, and also in acknowledging how selective he has been, this narrator reveals a great deal about himself as well as his father. What do we learn about the narrator from the details he chooses? If he had ended the description with the first paragraph, what different picture would we have of the father?

• • •

The girl they called Fat Maz worked in her father's newsagency. Her father had a club-foot and he was an angry man because the army had never wanted him. All day he clomped up and down between the racks of magazines keeping an eye out for thieves and making sure people bought things instead of standing and reading for free. The girl's mother sat all day at the register and watched the cars pass. Once a day the big Greyhound rolled past going north to the city. Only the dull drumming of the old National reminded the girl that her mother was there. She was always relieved when her parents went home for lunch and left the shop to her.

Every day at the lunch hour, a tall dark man came in, paused for a moment just inside the door as if to adjust his eyes or to get his bearings, before heading straight to the paperback novel called *Distant Lands*, opened it, and with his foot up on the bottom shelf, read for fifteen minutes. The first time he came in his reading was furtive; he spent as much time looking up to see if he was being watched as he did reading. His eyes showed white and worried over the burst of exotic purple on the cover, and to show that she couldn't have cared less, the girl smiled at him and shrugged.

'Interesting?' she asked that first day as he walked out without spending a cent.

The man said nothing. He just passed the register with his eyes downcast. When he got out into the street, he adjusted his tie, buttoned his jacket against the smelly harbour breeze, and went.

After that, the man came again, but he did not look at the girl or give any sign of recognition. Her father would have thrown him out. Not only was he freeloading; she guessed he was a Pakistani too. His Nescafé hands were clean and well-manicured. His suit was conservative and cut sharp. When she inspected *Distant Lands* she saw that he marked his place with a long, black hair. The book looked as though it had never been opened. On the back cover, the blurb said: *You will want this book never to finish.*

- From 'Distant Lands', Tim Winton in *Minimum of Two*, p. 67.

The whole set-up of this family and the moods of its three members comes across with minimal explanation or description. It all happens in the details: each one suggests whole stories that don't need to be told.

Think about the difference it would make if the first sentence didn't have the word 'they' in it. Think of how much her nickname tells us. Think of how much we learn about the father from the phrase 'because the Army had never wanted him'. The second time the register is mentioned it's called 'the old National' and the bus is the 'Greyhound'—what difference would it make if the brand names weren't used?

The writer could have told us in the first sentence that the man was wearing a suit and tie. What's the effect of introducing it in the way he does? The description of the man comes through the girl's consciousness: she notices his hands and his clothes but not his face or his whole bearing. What might that suggest about her, as well as him? The only figure-of-speech in this extract is 'Nescafé hands'— what extra resonances are given by the Nescafé image that wouldn't be if the writer had used 'coffee-coloured' or 'café-

au-lait' or 'pale brown' to describe the hands? Notice the
way in which we learn that the girl is curious about the
man; the reader is allowed to deduce it from watching her
actions rather than being told.

•••

1

A couple. A man and woman standing silent, as if
framed in a camera lens. Nothing moves. There is no
wind here to feather the smooth auburn of her hair. The
blue ice of his eyes seems flawless, unmeltable. Behind
them is a wall of smoky glass, with hints of further walls
and chambers beyond its dark translucency. Two low
archways, one on the left and one on the right, are open
at the corners of this wall. Another couple stand inside
the room, a man and woman. They too are still, facing
the first couple as if framed in a camera lens. Behind her
darkly glinting hair, and unobserved by his blue gaze, a
wall with two doorways grants shadowy glimpses of
further corridors and compartments. The two couples
stand, almost touching, separated by a veneer so thin it
might not be there. Yet this surface, transparent as air, is
the plane dividing two realities, or rather, dividing reality
from illusion. It is a mirror, for as one couple turn to face
each other, so too do their images. But which is the
living reality and which the reflection? Each woman
turns to face each man, each man turns to face each
woman. Their eyes meet quickly, watchfully, and yet
they might be strangers.

If they speak, go to 2.
If they don't speak, go to 3.

2

The man of each couple smiles. 'A frog he would a-
wooing go,' they laugh. 'We haven't been a-wooing,
Ruth. We've been amazing.' Their face becomes more
serious. 'You've been amazing.'

Now it is the woman of each pair who laughs. 'Naturally,' they say pertly. 'So now you must obey me. It's
time to go outside and get some sun.'

'Amazing,' the man intones, mock-reverent. And all
four figures leave the room, but only two escape the

mirror-maze to amble through the sunlight of the patterned garden. Behind them is a tall Palladian facade, its pilasters and pediments grafted to the stones of a more ancient manor. They stroll together hand-in-hand down pathways of heraldic topiary, past cooing columbaria, submerged in the scent and regimental finery of the serried flower-gardens. As if assembling piece by piece their own vignette, they sit beneath a beech tree and kiss with the easy intimacy of established lovers.

'Gerald wouldn't like that,' he says primly, then kisses her once more.

'Gerald wouldn't like a lot of things we've done this afternoon,' she replies.

• From 'Mirrors', Richard Lunn, in *Transgressions*, p. 3.

In this story, the main focus is not on realistic characters. Instead, our attention is constantly being drawn to the fact that these characters are pieces of fiction. As readers, we can watch the chessmaster, the writer, shifting his pawns around and inviting the reader to shift the order of events. If this piece is not aiming to create realistic characters, what do you think it might be aiming to do?

• • •

'Don't, but do not take everything I say *au pied de la lettre*.' Miss Hailey, towering in her formidable dressing gown, had additional height because of a round straw hat, Canadian Mounted Police style, with a narrow leather hat band a badge and a leather chin strap. She stopped to address Matron Price who was at her desk writing her report. Miss Hailey's eyes glowed, the hat made her feel efficient and knowledgeable. She would be able to tell someone the way if someone asked her.

'It is simply my great love of *la petite phrase*,' she said, '*la petite phrase*, I . . .'

'Yes. Yes! dear.' Hyacinth Price had been matron of The Hospital of St Christopher and St Jude for thirty years and had had Miss Hailey for ten of them and knew her for many more. 'Yes. Dear!' She looked up with a quick frown. She, in spite of Miss Hailey's support and faithfulness to St Christopher and St Jude, did not enjoy being leaned over especially while concentrating on the spelling of diarrhoea and haemorrhage. Both words, though repeatedly occurring in her life, gave her trouble. It was a sort of mental blockage, she told herself, probably a daily reminder that she needed a holiday in a remote place, on a peninsula or, better still, an island where neither could exist. Though it was likely that some other difficult word would turn up even there, and she'd be unable to spell it. A word like archipelago for instance. She was not sure how to pronounce it let alone spell it.

Here I am in the Greek Islands, the archipelago...
How could she even send a post card from her holiday if unable to write the word,
food good, weather splendid, the arkipalargo very lovely...
She began to try the word out on the blotting paper. Her pen hovered, caressing the fast-spreading ink.

'Yes, I'll go and lie down. I think I am a little tired,' Miss Hailey replied, from habit, to a suggestion Miss Price no longer needed to make aloud.

• From *Mr Scobie's Riddle*, Elizabeth Jolley, p. 12.

Elizabeth Jolley's fiction is full of characters who aren't particularly 'lifelike', in the sense of being like people we meet every day. Yet these characters are entirely convincing within the pages of her fiction.

This extract is only quite short, but in it Jolley uses many different devices in order to build a strongly drawn picture of her characters: physical description, dialogue, interior thoughts, letters and information conveyed directly by the narrator.

Think how different the first sentence would be if it was 'Don't take everything I say literally'. What is the extra that we get from the way Jolley has written it? Would the description of the hat lose something if it was simply 'a round hat of the kind Canadian Mounted Police wear'? The very close scrutiny of the details helps to normalise this odd item. In a complementary way, describing the dressing-gown (usually a banal item) as 'formidable' gives it a strangeness that makes it significant.

We see the hat through our own eyes in the description, and feel it to be outlandish. However, in the next paragraph we see how the character responds to it. Her feelings are entirely logical. Wearing that hat makes her feel the opposite of outlandish — she feels competent and responsible. It's a Mountie's hat; it's logical that it makes her feel like a Mountie. We are led to share her logic, so that although she remains 'odd' she is no longer incomprehensible. Think, though, how differently we'd feel about her if the author had put these ideas in the form of explanation rather than the character's own thoughts: 'Wearing the hat made Miss Hailey feel competent and knowledgeable.' Would there be the same feeling of sharing her logic?

The stream-of-consciousness of Hyacinth Price's thoughts leads her from a perfectly ordinary difficulty with spelling into an elaborate fantasy involving imaginary postcards from imaginary Greek islands. As with Miss Hailey's hat, the use of the character's own thoughts encourages the reader to swim along with the character rather than judge from a distance. The device of the postcards, using words the character would choose to write, is another way of learning about her.

In the last two sentences of the extract, we learn not just about the relationship of these characters at this moment, but also something of their entire history together. This history is present in this moment: we can understand it very clearly without needing it to be spelled out.

•••

> She heaves herself out of the grubby heap of bedclothes, her flannel nightie rucking up above the enormously fat white legs, a glimpse of grizzled pubic hair between the rolls of abdomen and thigh. She gropes for under-clothes, puts on her pants and the huge brassiere before taking off the tent-like gown.
>
> She picks up a vest, a jumper and pair of cut down men's longjohns from the floor where she always steps out of them, and slowly puts them on. Last the soiled and sweat-stained blue serge sack — she looks at it, it will do another day — and struggles until finally she is covered from neck to elbows to mid calf. She shuffles into the wrecked slippers and goes outside to the wash house, where she wipes a flannel over her face, neck and hands. She ties her wiry bun behind her fat-creased neck. She doesn't look into the mirror above the basin. She moves painfully on down the dirt path to the dunny and settles gratefully for a long and relieving time.

The yard is piled with crates and fruit boxes. Heaps of old vegetables decompose against the far fence. The dogs come out from under the house to sniff around outside the dunny, waiting for her morning growl and their bones. The heifers push their tender noses against the fence, nuzzling at the cabbages on top of the heaps of compost. She will come straight to them and mutter softly, pushing at their gentle faces, calling them by name, caressing them, crooning to their mothers as they wander single file down the hill path to be milked.

When her nephew arrives to do the milking she goes inside to get the old man his morning cup of tea. She goes about this slowly, grunting occasionally as she reaches for milk, sugar and sweet biscuits. When she has loaded the tray she goes to wake her decrepit old father.

She shakes him awake, muttering the time, that her feet are hurting, she needs new corn plasters, tells him to drink his tea while it's still hot, gets him his wash-basin and cloth and picks up his chamberpot from beneath the bed. She walks out to throw the reeking contents into the toilet bowl, plods back with it and leaves him. She will look in at him again in a few hours when she has unpacked the new cases of fruit and topped up the boxes already stacked in the shed.

• • •

Hazel claimed the more beautiful of the sisters was Bella. She was a creamy fullblown Edwardian maiden with drooping shadowed eyes and a soft slender neck. Her thick hair was piled to the top of her head, held with a tortoiseshell comb. In a lacy long dress, held tightly around the waist by a ribbon, with her powdered burgeoning bosom, she looked, the girls sniggered, as if she'd do it alright. They were all lovely, those women in sepia photographs and she was one of the loveliest.

• From *Country Girl Again*, Jean Bedford, pp 1–2, 6.

This is an example of character in action, a gradual process of moving out from a close-up on a character in isolation to an image of her in her whole social context.

First Bedford gives us a few basic facts: what Isabella looks like and what she wears. In the next paragraph we see some of her environment and watch how she is with animals: this modifies the impression those first images created. Next we watch her making a cup of tea, and her particular way of going about this adds to our picture of her. Finally we see her with another person, and having a conversation: the two-dimensional picture of the first sentence has been enriched and broadened so that Bella is now a complex character inhabiting a convincingly evoked world.

Watching Bella like this, in action, reveals one dimension of her character. In the last paragraph of this extract there's a shift in point of view. From p. 6 on, we see Bella through the eyes of a young girl who is looking at a photo of Bella when she was young and lovely. The two images side by side set up a powerful incongruity. Another dimension of the characterisation is taking place in the gap between the image of the present and the image of the past.

T HERE are four basic groups of exercises here. You will begin by writing about a real person from life, and progressively move further and further into transforming that person into a character in fiction.

1 A person

The most obvious thing about a person is the way they look, so we'll start with that. The way a person looks is not very interesting in itself, but it's interesting if it lets us guess at something of what they're like.

Glance through your fragments from Chapter 1. If any of them were about a real person whom you know reasonably well (but not yourself), you could use that person as the basis for this exercise. Otherwise, think of someone you know — a friend or neighbour, perhaps.

3.1 Describe this person in terms of their appearance: their physical characteristics, the way they dress, the way they move, objects they might have around themselves, such as cigarettes or a parasol. These are all external facts about this person and some of them will have no particular significance. For example, if a person has brown hair, that probably doesn't tell us anything more than that physical fact. However, some of the items you've mentioned will represent something about the inner life, the personality, of the person you've described. For example, if their hair is green, something about their inner life is being expressed, though it mightn't be clear exactly what. Go through your description and mark the items that might be a clue to personality. One test is whether you can ask the question 'why' about something you've mentioned.

Now look at the items that aren't clues to anything. Given that you know the personality of this person, is there any way you could change these inexpressive details so that they, too, become clues to personality?

49

3.2 Go through and re-write the description with this in mind. At the same time, see if there's anything else you can make up that might be a further clue to personality. Your real person might not have any particular mannerisms that express personality, so try inventing some. One way to make this easier is to borrow from another real person. Think about the people you know and see if you can put together a patchwork of characteristics in order to create this new portrait. See if you can end up with a description in which everything mentioned is some sort of indicator of the person's inner life. This may be a rather over-laden description but this is only an exercise, not a finished character.

Looking at the description you have now, you've probably become aware of one of the problems with descriptions of people: the 'grocery-list' effect, where all the characteristics are strung together in a mechanical way that becomes numbing to read. But a grocery list is a good place to start, and here's one way to start making the list less mechanical:

3.3 Take one detail from the description you have and use it as the basis for an improvisation. Write the detail at the top of a page and then ask the question 'why' about it until you've written a paragraph or two. Although your description is based on someone you know, you may not quite know the answer to the question 'why'. All the better: invent!

Starting with a person you know well has the advantage that you're working from something you know towards the areas where you have to guess or invent. Now let's reverse this process, because that's a way of finding out other kinds of things.

3.4 Write a physical portrait of a stranger you've seen recently: in the street, on a bus, in the supermarket. Write everything you can remember, whether or not it seems significant: just the fact that you remembered it makes it significant.

Now use these physical facts as the basis for questions. Why does their hair look the way it does? Why are they wearing those clothes? Why are they carrying that object? Why do they have that expression on their face? Branch out more and more widely with further questions: where have they just been, where are they going, what did they do a week ago, what will they be doing next week, what was their childhood like, what are their close relationships, what sort of environment do they live in?

It's fairly easy to come up with plausible guesses about people, so your first set of answers may be rather predictable. Once you've guessed the obvious, try guessing at the surprising: see what other answers you could come up with for the same questions.

2 Person becomes character
With that first exercise you began the movement away from a literal portrait of a person. These exercises go further in that direction.

3.5   Go back to the portrait of the person you know (exercise 3.2). Think of another characteristic — not one that the real person has. Look at your 'piles' from Chapter 2 and see if there's a character there with some quirk you could use here. For example, I might choose my traveller and use his foreignness as the characteristic to focus on. Rewrite your description so that it incorporates the quirk you've identified. Some things from your original description will have to be changed, others deleted and new ones might need to be added.

What you have now is no longer a person with an existence in real life: this is now a character. What you have now is a piece of fiction. As the creator of this character, you know some things about him or her but other things remain blanks. Now you can discover, and invent, what might be in those blank areas.

As you do the following exercise, keep in mind what you already know about this character but don't let that stop you going off in another direction if it seems interesting. In the course of discovering more about him or her, you might find your initial description wasn't quite on target.

3.6 Sketch out a biography of this character. This might include: childhood, home life, work, close relationships, family, pets, relations with neighbours.

Now describe their environment: where they live or where they work, or both. What personal things have they got there?

Describe a typical day in their life, from waking to going to sleep. It may become evident that this character has no typical days, in which case you could describe what they did yesterday.

Remember, all this is just exploration. In a final piece of writing you might not use any of this background to your character. But as the writer, you should know it even if the reader doesn't.

We're starting to know a good bit about the external facts of this character but the most interesting things about both characters and people are their feelings. Let's give this character some feelings now.

3.7 Start with one of the facts you now know about the character and write a paragraph or two about how the character feels about that fact. For example, they might live in a top-floor flat but would really like to live in a small, wooden cottage with a garden. They might have spent their life trying to make their curly hair straight or their straight hair curly.

Feeling is a good motor to get writing going. This is all the more true when the feeling belongs to you, the writer. It's sometimes hard to invent an emotion for a character but you may be able to borrow one of your own that might be made to fit.

Feeling is a source of great energy in writing, but writing directly about feeling often doesn't work. One way to get the most out of the energy locked into feeling is to put the feeling inside a character, rather than to try to write about the feeling itself.

3.8   Think of something that's happened to you recently that's made you feel strongly. The feeling might be embarrassment or anger or joy or depression. Now give that event and that feeling to your character. Write a short account of the event as if it happened to your character and let your character experience the emotions.

In doing this exercise you might have discovered the limitations of transferring your own emotions directly into fiction. You may find that the character you've created might not be suited to your events and your feelings. Try this:

3.9   Take the same feeling but give the character a completely different cause for it. You might be enraged by the cynicism of politicians. Your character might be enraged at the way the man in front is driving.
   Write a short account of what has made your character feel the way he or she does, and describe the feelings as the character experiences them.

Giving the emotions to a character lets you express them to the full: since they belong to someone else, they can be as unreasonable as you like and can be exaggeratedly angry, ironic, sad or funny. You can use all the energy of your own feeling but it has a channel to flow through that will make the fiction stronger rather than weaker.

3 Character in action
You now have a character but there's still a lot about this character that you haven't discovered. So far this has been a very static portrait of a character and there's a limit to what you can discover unless the character can be put in motion. How do you get characters to move?

53

3.10 You might begin by giving them something simple to do. Take your character and describe him or her making a cup of tea or walking down a flight of stairs or waiting for someone. What is your character like with a dog? How does your character cook a meal? How does your character organise a party or drive a car?

Everyone does these simple things slightly differently and expresses something of their personality in the way they do it. Your character will do the same.

Up to now, we've only learnt about this character through you, the narrator, telling us about him or her. Now it's time to hear the character's own voice.

3.11 Go back to the account of your character doing some simple activity such as making a cup of tea. Rather than just watching the character, this time let's listen to what he or she is thinking while the tea is being made. Describe the activity again, starting with the word 'I'.

You might have the character write a letter to someone or describe himself or herself to us.

This is the character describing himself or herself. The way the character looks at other characters will reveal a great deal, too.

3.12 Get your character to describe the person you described in exercise 3.4: the stranger at the bus-stop. Your character may view this person rather differently. Your character may notice things you didn't notice, and your character may bring a different set of judgements to the person. The description that your character writes of the bus-stop person might be much more sympathetic than yours was, or it might be much less so.

Write a description of the bus-stop person from your character's point of view and see how much you can make the character reveal about himself or herself in what is chosen or ignored.

What people say is important but how they say it is even more important. Do the last two exercises sound like the voice your character would be likely to have, or is it still your voice? Would the character use words differently, be more or less formal, more or less grammatical, and would the character use comparisons and idioms that you might not?

3.12 Re-write the last exercise, trying to make the character's voice as convincing as possible and different from your voice.

That was the voice of the character speaking directly to the reader. Now, the ultimate test for your new-born character: get them to speak with another character.

3.13 Write a short account of your character meeting the bus-stop person. What is their relationship, if any? They might kiss or shake hands or look away. They might be pleased or angry or embarrassed. Now, engage them in conversation. Let it go wherever it leads you: this is another kind of improvisation.

You might come to a dead end too quickly, depending on your original choices. If you come to a dead end or if it gets predictable or dull, start again with a different choice. If you try a few, one of them is sure to be interesting.

4 Manipulating the reader

Usually, though not always, readers have a feeling about the characters they're reading about: they like them or hate them, trust them or distrust them or vary in their feelings from page to page. In this sense fiction is like life.

But in an important way, fiction is different from life. In life, events just flow along; in fiction they're shaped to a purpose. That purpose is present, no matter how foggily, in the writer's mind and dictates the choices that the writer makes, many of them unconscious ones. A writer chooses to mention one fact about the character but not another, chooses to describe one set of characteristics rather than another set that would be equally convincing. This means that the reader is only seeing the character through the filter of the writer's mind.

So, willy-nilly the writer is manipulating the reader, in the sense that the reader only knows what the writer is revealing. Since manipulation can't be avoided — it is, in fact, what writing *is* and why writing is different from life — a writer has to learn to be in control of that manipulation. A writer has to learn to make choices that will subtly direct the reader towards the writer's larger purpose.

The writer has two tools for directing the reader: what is described and how it is described. The previous exercises have covered the ground of what is described. Now we come to how it's described.

3.14 Go back to your description from exercise 3.1. Imagine that in the wider framework of your purpose, you want this character to be disliked by the reader. Re-write the description, using the same details but expressing them in an unfavourable way. For example, in the original description the character's hair might have been described as 'very curly' which is a value-free statement. You could change that to 'messy' or 'uncared-for', which would load the description with a negative attitude.

Now reverse the process. Use all the same items in the description but load them with favourable bias. The 'very curly' hair might now be 'lustrous curls' or 'an exuberant mass of hair'.

Building your story

L ET's see now how all this can be applied to the material you've already written. Whether you're working with your embryonic story from Chapter 2, or a previously written story that you're re-working, you can do the same things.

For the moment, forget everything about your material except the characters. Write out a list of all the characters who appear, including the narrator if it's first-person writing. You probably have one or two main characters and a number of minor ones. For the moment, treat them all as equally important. It often happens that a story seems to be about one character, but the real centre of interest is someone else altogether. When you come to a dead end with a story, it's sometimes because you're concentrating on the wrong character.

Knowing what you now know about making characters, apply some of the exercises you've just done to each of your characters. For example, try describing them physically in some detail. Try describing their environment and write an account of a typical day for them. Sketch their life-history.

Now take two or three of your characters and make them interact in some way. It may not be in the way you originally thought: give the characters plenty of freedom to surprise you. Don't worry at this point about the story, just give the characters their heads. If they start to get carried away, let them. If a minor character lets loose an avalanche of ideas, go with it. If the whole thing starts to go off in some unexpected direction, follow it. Your unconscious mind may have a plan which your conscious mind can't yet see.

Now use the idea of piles again. Go through all the new material from this chapter. Which bits do you find dull? Which bits are funny, or vivid, or make you want to find out more? Which bits seem to have come to a dead end, and which could you go on writing about?

Now go back to your original ideas: either your embryonic story from Chapter 2 or the old story you're re-working. Add to this original material any of these new piles that seem interesting.

All this work on characters will probably mean that the original story has changed. Someone who seemed a minor character then might have emerged now as a major character. The relationships between the characters might have changed. Several new characters may have entered the story, perhaps replacing original ones. A new character might be able to be combined with an original one.

The change might be even more radical than this. You might find that everything you wrote before is less interesting than what you've just written. You may decide to put the whole of the original material on the back burner and go in a new direction entirely.

You may find that you can use some of this new material about characters just as you wrote it, or you may find that it needs to be adapted before it can be used in the story. You may find that you don't use it at all but that it provides background depth for the story: you, as the writer understand your characters better and you can choose whether or not to let the reader know all that you know.

This might all seem a very roundabout way of getting a story happening. Experience with writing can streamline the process somewhat but writing is nearly always a matter of trial and error, of false starts and dead ends. There's no shortcut to doing it well but none of the exploration is a waste of time, though it may sometimes seem to be; the discoveries are only possible because of the exploration.

Creating characters out of bits and pieces from many sources is all about manipulating the reader by shaping the way the information is presented. Behind the facts and the incidents, the description and the details, there is an attitude, a 'point of view', and this is what the next chapter will look at in detail.

4 Point of View

POINT of view isn't an optional extra in a story. Every
piece of writing, no matter how neutral it seems, has
a point of view. This is because there's no way of
transmitting information directly from one brain into another. In between, there are always words. The person
using the words is choosing one way of saying it rather than
another—and those choices add up to 'point of view'.

The person using the words is always the writer, of
course. But writers don't always tell the story in their own
voice. They might use a narrator and borrow his or her
voice. The narrator is often a character out of the story, but
the narrator can also be a faceless story-teller. With or
without a face and a name, the voice of the narrator affects
the story.

What is 'point of view'?

Point of view can become a confusing technical problem.
Points of view can be endlessly categorised, from 'first-
person limited' to 'dramatic third-person omniscient' and
everywhere in between.

A more practical way of thinking about point of view is to
ask these questions about the piece:
- who's telling this story
- how much do they know

- are they telling the truth?

— Point of view is the voice a story speaks with, so it has to be the right voice for the right story. That's where it's useful to look at the range that's possible, because the point of view in which you first write your story might not be the most dramatic point of view for it. Point of view can go on changing through different drafts as a story reveals itself more fully to the writer.

It's tempting, when writing stories about things that happened to you, to write in the first person. The stories might come out that way the first time, but as finished pieces they might be more powerful told from another point of view.

The choices

Point of view can be paralysing if you think about it too early. For the first draft or two, write in whatever point of view comes naturally, or in many different ones if that's what comes out. Worry later about choosing a consistent point of view.

English grammar lets us write in three ways:
- in the first person, using an 'I' narrator,
- in the third person, describing everyone as 'he' or 'she',
- in the second person, 'you'.

First person

A story told in the first person has the limitations, and the strengths, of being filtered through the consciousness of 'I'. This means that an 'I' narrator can only know about events he or she saw. Otherwise the narrator has to rely on what other people said.

An 'I' narrator needs to establish its authority for telling the story. Was the narrator actually there? If not, how does the narrator know so much? Is the narrator putting together evidence from somewhere else: what other people have said, letters found in an attic, messages in bottles? Or is the narrator just guessing?

Also, an 'I' narrator tends to become a personality: it's an individual speaking directly to the reader, and a character in the story. So the reader tries to build up a picture of that 'I': what is 'I' like? Do we like 'I'?

An 'I' narrator is likely to have an axe to grind in the story because 'I' was involved in it, even if only as an observer, or as the person who put all the evidence together. In that case, what motive does 'I' have for telling the story? Does this narrator just want to get to the truth? Or does the narrator want to talk us into something? Can 'I' be trusted to tell the truth? Look at the example from *Reasons for Going into Gynaecology*, p. 67, where the narrator is at pains to convince us that he's right, and compare with the extract from *Illywhacker*, where the narrator is at pains to tell us that he is a liar.

The kind of language a first-person narrator might use depends on who 'I' is. This is not to say that the language needs to match up with the type of character in a stereo-typed way: a first-person narrator who was a child wouldn't necessarily have to tell the story in childish language. But a child 'I' using adult language would need to be made convincing to the reader: it's another factor the writer has to be aware of. To get an idea about language use, look at *The Bodysurfers* extract, pp. 64–65. First person can give a force, an immediacy, an idiosyncratic and personal energy to a piece of writing. Look at the extract from 'Neons', p.69.

First-person narrators are limited, then, but limitations in fiction are not always a bad thing. The story may be more interesting, more dramatic, if it's told by someone who doesn't know the full story, or who gets it wrong, or who isn't telling the truth. The limitations of first person can be exactly what a story needs.

Third person
Sometimes a third-person narrator can be almost as personal as a first person, and have the same sort of limitations. If we want to get technical about it, this is often called 'third-person subjective'. For an example of a highly personal, third-person narrator, see the extract from *For Love Alone*, p. 70.

At the other extreme, a third-person narrator can be a God-like voice who knows everything and is equally in the heads of all the characters: 'Third-person omniscient'. Look at the piece from *Riders in the Chariot*, pp. 71–72 and, for a different version of the God-like narrator, look at the extract from *Buttercup and Wendy*, p. 8–9.

Third person can lack the intimacy of first person, the

sense the reader has of identifying with the narrator. On the other hand, a third-person narrative can be enriched by its flexibility—a third-person narrator can go anywhere, do anything, know everything.

Second person

Using second person is a challenge. It's very limited in knowledge, and over an extended piece it's unsettling for the reader. It can start to sound rather bullying or it can force you to identify with a character you feel very much at odds with. There can be an overpowering intimacy about second-person writing. See the first extract from from *The Frangipani Gardens*, p. 73.

These qualities can make the writing very powerful, although over a long piece the reader may need some relief. See how Hanrahan solves this problem in the second extract from *The Frangipani Gardens*, pp. 73–74.

Consistent point of view

Point of view is the frame within which the story happens, so if the frame suddenly changes shape to include more or less of the story, it can be disconcerting. You may wish to use that as a deliberate effect. But if you don't, you should check that it is just one frame, not several, that you've placed around the story.

Third-person narrators of the God-like kind are free to be anywhere and to be in the minds of all the characters. But 'limited' points of view are based on the idea that the narrator is speaking out of one particular mind. Problems in consistency can arise with a limited point of view; the reader becomes used to seeing the story through one mind but suddenly the story 'hops over' into another mind and starts telling it from another point of view.

Ask the questions: who is telling this story, and would they know what they're telling us at this moment. If they don't know from their own direct experience, but are just guessing, how can I, the writer, let the reader know whether the narrator is guessing correctly?

D UTIFULLY following Horne's Rule of Diligence —
Miss nothing and take one of everything — I was
embarrassed to find that I was the first to arrive at the
conference auditorium on the first day, and stood about
like a new boy.

Half seriously, Horne's Rule of commitment-to-the-
total-experience helped overcome the temptation to skip
a paper because I'd 'heard it all before' or to linger over
lunch and slide into afternoon drinking. Predictions
about papers were always partially wrong. Usually
something unexpected in the most predictable of occasions, I used the rule, too, to take me into social
situations which I might have backed out of. It yielded
some rewards, the undoctored experience — and also led
me into a lot of wasted and tiresome times.

So I was the first to register. I felt a bit of the too-early
fool. I went through the ritual of joining. I picked up my
lapel identification tag, my plastic satchel, my revised
program, my ticket to the buffet. A ballpoint pen with
the conference theme printed on it. A TAA survival
kit' — toothbrush, map, soap, and so on. I didn't need
it, but I took one of everything. They were presents.
Accoutrements.

A worried man and a harried woman wearing a badge
saying *Official Welcomer*, were too harried and worried
to welcome me.

I put my things on or about me. Together with my
personal equipage I was a little over-loaded. I found my
way to a seat in the empty auditorium, empty except for
an official adjusting a microphone. I dumped everything
on the desk. I realised I had all sorts of things about me.
Protectively surrounded. Reports, tissues, chewing
gum, Codral. A hip flask — carried for use in the ultimate personal catastrophe when there was only one
possible exit — drunkenness.

• From *Conference-ville*, Frank Moorhouse, p. 21

Because of the way this narrator describes himself, we tend to sympathise with him, but it would be possible to imagine the same character described in a very unsympathetic way, if written from a different point of view. What is it in the way he describes himself that makes him sympathetic? What changes would you make, to transform this into an unsympathetic account of him?

Even in this short extract there are several long lists of items. What's the effect of these lists? Do you find this piece funny? What is it about the choice of words that makes it so?

• • •

I get the 8.15 bus from the station and I'm on the beach by nine. I usually take my camera and a good pair of Jap binoculars, a bit of lunch, a magazine and a couple of those little cardboard packs of Milo with the drinking straw attached. One of the new-fangled things I do like since I got out is the way they have these little cardboard packs of juice and what-have-you that you stack in the fridge. Even Milo now. I like my Milo. Before I went inside it only came in those green tins with a bloke carrying a bull on his back. Milo was hard to get inside. Plenty of tea full of pieces of twig and hessian bag and horse shit for all I know, and a jar of Nescafé if you buy it with your laundry wage, but Milo, no. I whack all this in a plastic bag and I'm off for the day.

As you'd expect, when I first got out I was all over the place like a mad woman's lunchbox. Sex on my mind the whole time, racing from one beach to another, must have trudged over every sandhill in the state! Now I mostly concentrate on the one beach. Don't think I'm going to give the beach away! They've got these sort of vigilante groups now and they come at you all fury and saggy balls, not even stopping to put their pants on, with the intention of beating the shit out of you. They really get them in a knot. A few times I ran for it but I got wise in my old age. Now if they see the sun glinting off the binoculars and scramble up the sandhills after me, by the time they get to me I'm reading my *TV Week*, sipping my Milo.

'What're you doing, you bloody pervert?' they say. Insults don't hurt me in the slightest. 'I beg your pardon, mate,' I say. 'I beg your pardon.' I act a bit put out but not aggressive. If you stand on your dignity people lose their nerve and shuffle around. It's hard to be belligerent with no pants on. After a while they go back to their volleyball.

> • From 'The View from the Sandhills', in
> *The Bodysurfers*, Robert Drewe, p. 88

It's interesting to try to pinpoint just what the clues are in this extract that make the reader's view of this character diverge from the character's view of himself: where irony begins to happen. This extract begins by setting up a series of innocent, humble images: the bus, the beach, Milo. There's only one slightly odd note here: the 'good pair of Jap binoculars'. Who is telling this story? Someone pretty harmless. How much does he know? The unexplained detail of the binoculars is a clue that he knows more than he's saying. Is he telling the truth? There are no clues so far that he isn't.

The mention of Milo, such an innocent childish thing in itself, is the device whereby we learn in the second paragraph that this man's been in prison. It's just information at this stage, but it gives a radical shift to the context that affects everything else. The fact that he chooses to tell us in this casual way reinforces the feeling that he knows more than he's telling and can just as easily keep such details concealed. The narrator clearly knows more than the reader in this case.

The phrase 'As you'd expect' at the start of the third paragraph invites sympathy with what comes next and is followed by unassuming, unthreatening images: the funny simile, the disarming image of him 'racing' or 'trudging' over beaches: there's an invitation to see him as a bit of a figure of fun. The sentence 'Now I mostly concentrate...' abruptly drops that tone: it's down to serious business. But what business? You get the feeling this narrator's enjoying the game of teasing the reader with hints, but delaying the moment of telling us just what's going on.

'Don't think I'm going to give the beach away!' Until this point, the narrator has used various devices to invite us to identify with him. This sentence suddenly puts a barricade up. The relationship with the reader now has a hint of competition, even antagonism. It raises the question whether he is telling the truth. If he wants to keep some things hidden, what else might he be hiding?

Now that he's put some distance between himself and us with this sentence, we now read the narrative with less total identification with his point of view. Now the language is more aggressive, too: 'They've got these sort of vigilante groups now and they come at you all fury and saggy balls, not even stopping to put their pants on, with the intention of beating the shit out of you.' This is very far from the language of the harmless bloke with his Milo. Our idea of 'Who is telling this story' has undergone a radical shift from the first paragraph.

On the other hand, look at the word 'you'. It's used twice in this sentence, and it makes it harder to resist identifying with the narrator—it's become 'us' that's being chased by the vigilantes. Point of view is forcing the reader into a very complex reading experience—identifying at the same time as distrusting.

In the second-last paragraph there's a replay of the mild-mannered, Milo-drinking image, but we know more than we did the first time so it's heavily ironic this time around. The question 'How much does he know' has shifted, too: he knows more than the vigilantes, and so does the reader. By the narrator's sharing his private knowledge, the reader is a kind of accomplice to what he's doing. In another context our sympathies might be with the vigilantes. But in the context of this point of view, we're forced to see them ironically, and to share to some extent the narrator's view of them as fools.

The last paragraph shows the final irony: not only is this bloke not an innocent old codger, but it's actually a role he adopts with cool cynicism. Who is telling this story? Certainly not the harmless bloke we thought at the beginning. How much does he know? Within these events, he knows everything, even down to knowing just how to manipulate the reader, as well as the volley-ball players. Is he telling the truth? Looking back, we can see how he's concealed the truth, or revealed it, just as it suited him. Why shouldn't there be another layer of truth behind what he's chosen to tell us?

Imagine this piece written in the third person. Would the irony still work? This piece demonstrates a kind of seduction by point of view into identification, to some extent, with someone we wouldn't normally identify with. It's a masterfully complex use of the enforced intimacy of first-person point of view.

• • •

She keeps mincing through the room. Her heels, stupidly high for the house, clatter backwards and forwards, spitting out pique and inarticulate frustration and intense dislike. The mood could, of course, be transformed in a moment. But I'm no longer interested in doing so. She goes from bathroom to suitcase to cupboard to suitcase, unnecessary, reduplicated journeys most of them, brandishing her departure in front of me. She hopes, transparently, that I'll stand up, yank her by the wrist as she goes past, tell her to stop the nonsense, and to sit down. But I'm watching porn, fairly soft porn, on the video, and I'm not even tempted to dwell on her pathetic charade. I imagine she looks at the film when she's behind me. She would say it's only curiosity. I would say that's crap. I would say she's a little tramp and would make a sly grab for whatever she can get. But she's cute enough not to let her step falter.

'Instructions for the nappy wash are on your desk,' she says on one of these ghost-train irruptions.

I refuse to acknowledge her. Tomorrow she goes to LA—it would have to be LA of course with her—and straight into the pants of this stud she's picked up.

'The cats are due for their operation,' she tries. 'Unless of course you're going to do it yourself.'

I'm impervious. I should get close to six months' peace. As the Puerto Rican rooster loses his appeal, she's likely to discover her maternal instincts again, and head for home.

• From 'Reasons for Going into Gynaecology',
Gerard Windsor, in
Memories of the Assassination Attempt, p. 27.

This narrator is absolutely sure that he's right, and that his interpretation of things is the only correct one. Because it's a first-person story, the reader tends to go along with his view to some extent. But there are things that make us wonder whether he's right, and to distance ourselves from the narrator: to doubt the accuracy of his point of view. In this extract, in contrast to the extract by Drewe, the reader may know more than the narrator, because the reader, unlike the narrator, can see that there might be another side to this story.

At the start of the piece the reader is on the side of the narrator because there's nothing to indicate that his judgement isn't reliable. But when the narrator mentions how he might 'yank her by the wrist', and tells us that he's watching porn as his wife packs, our view shifts. It becomes clear that the narrator is not just innocently sitting as a spectator of his wife's actions: there's an undercurrent of violence and provocation.

In the first sentences of the extract, the narrator interpreted his wife's actions for us: he speculated that she was hoping he'd stop her leaving. We might have gone along with his interpretation then, but perhaps now, knowing how provocative he's being, we might not trust his interpretation so willingly. In the last few sentences of this paragraph, the narrator presents what he thinks his wife is thinking ('She would say it's only curiosity'), only in order to demolish her response. Knowing what we know now about him, we might wonder if he's interpreting her thoughts correctly.

When we learn that his wife is not just leaving him, but leaving him for a 'stud' in L.A., it makes sense of his vitriol. This is a man with his back to the wall, emotionally. So, when he claims that he's looking forward to six months peace, his claim could have a slightly hollow ring to it.

The use of point of view in this story allows room for the complexity and contradictory nature of human feelings. The reader is always in the position of considering whether the truth might be the opposite of what the narrator says it is. In the reader's mind, if not in the narrator's, there's a complicated play of sympathies that allows more than one thing to be true simultaneously. The narrator might be genuinely pleased to see his wife go, and he might at the same time be bluffing to cover distress. Both these possibilities are present, without ever being resolved, through the adroit use of a limited and possibly unreliable point of view.

•••

light me bright me match me cigarette me bright city
turn on be loud tell everybody switch yes sing red pencil
tick me to on centre mid town go go glow sky lit lines
wire buzz me to see ring on me in neon on heady excite
me thrill me hold me to tight rush rush be big loud go
right through now leap nerve me beat drums loud
louder fast run fast right now once go places all the time
eat more restaurant flash me show me lively dance put
lipstick on neons all colour zap me power lines shine
letter light big n me blow me put high fast see me watch
zing my string best bouncy tube glow in me get ready
do it now don't wait hurry get it right first time do it
once no again switch me on i travel fast light switch me
on pink candy say words loud-speaker my microphone
leap high as can big city centre city big very buildings
whole wide world hot lights on stage line my eyes
breathe deep all revved up fast car go fast car go fast
good kill somebody dress to top fashion strut get them
wiggle pink face daze me amaze me shine me neons on
sweet buzz meter

• From 'Neons', Ania Walwicz, in *Transgressions*, p. 84.

This first-person narrator is not so much narrating as
singing; but the choice of point of view gives the song a
particular quality. There is an intimacy about this 'I' speaking to an implied 'you' who is the reader. Imagine what a
difference a shift of point of view would make:

> . . . light her bright her match her cigarette her bright city
> turn on be loud tell everybody switch yes sing red pencil
> tick her to on centre midtown . . .

And the piece would change again if it no longer used the
imperative form of the verb:

> . . . he lights her he brights her he matches her he ciga-
> rettes her . . .

It's interesting to look at other possibilities to see how
well Walwicz's version works. By fracturing language as

69

Walwicz does, she forces the reader into a close look at each word and reveals new possibilities in the ways they might go together. By breaking language down into small units, her writing suggests new and startling ways of putting it back together. Walwicz makes us notice every word, whereas the usual reading experience is a flow in which individual words are blurred.

•••

> Standing upright at the window, thinking, thinking, feeling rage at her floundering and weakness, and at seeing all the issues blocked, she thought of how cocksure she had been at school. Awkward, easily faced down, of course, but confident about the future. The things she wanted existed. At school she first had news of them, she knew they existed; what went on round her was hoaxing and smooth-faced hypocrisy. Venus and Adonis, the Rape of Lucrece, Troilus and Cressida were reprinted for three hundred years, St Anthony was tempted in the way you would expect; Dido, though a queen, was abandoned like a servant-girl and went mad with love and grief, like the girl in the boat outside. This was the truth, not the daily simpering on the boat and the putting away in hope chests; but where was one girl who thought so, besides herself? Was there one who would not be afraid if she told them the secret, the real life? Since school, she had ravaged libraries, disembowelled hundreds of books, ranged through literature since the earliest recorded frenzies of the world and had eaten into her few years with this boundless love of love, this insensate thirst for the truth above passion, alive in their home itself, in her brothers and sister, but neglected, denied, and useless; obnoxious in school, workshop, street.
> • From *For Love Alone*, Christina Stead, p. 75.

This is an example of 'third-person subjective' — it's third person, but it's very much through the mind of one character.

One of the differences might be in the authority of the narrative voice. A first-person account might be unreliable: the narrator of this extract in the first person could simply be slightly mad. The use of third person lends more authority to the judgements being made; we're likely to trust that voice where we might question a first-person voice. The narrator is not the character, but a voice which is outside the story while knowing everything that goes on within it. There would need to be strong signals to cause us to distrust the judgements of this third-person narrator.

• • •

After several years of tedious and frustrated childbirth, Mrs Hare had succeeded in having this little girl. They named her Mary, because the mother, fortunately, was too exhausted to think, and the father, who would have plunged with voluptuous excitement into the classics, or the works of Tennyson, to dredge up some shining name for a son, turned his back on the prospect of a daughter. So Mary the latter became, but an innocent Protestant one.

Mrs Hare had soon taken refuge from Mary in a rational kindness, with which she continued to deal her a series of savage blows during what passed for childhood.

'My darling must decide how best she can repay her parents for all she owes them,' was amongst the mother's favourite tactics. 'See all these beautiful things they have put here to be enjoyed, not smashed in thoughtless games.'

And, in answer to a frequent question:

'Only our Father in Heaven will be able to tell my pet why He made her as he did.'

Paddling in her own delicious shallows, it never occurred to Mrs Hare to raise her eyes to God, except to call Him as a formal witness. She accepted Him—who would have been so audacious not to?—but as the creator of a moral and a social system. At that level, she could always be relied on to put her hand in her purse, to help repair vestments, or support fallen girls, and her name was published for everyone to read, on a visiting card, inserted in a brass frame, on the end of her regular pew.

The little girl appeared gravely to accept the attitudes adopted by her mother, but was not genuinely influenced. Unattached, she drifted through the pale waters of her mother's kindness like a little, wondering, trans-

> parent fish, in search of those depths which her instinct told her could exist.
> • From *Riders in the Chariot*, Patrick White, p. 21

This third-person narrator is not solely in the mind of one character, as the narrator in the Stead extract was. This narrator takes a much more distanced view of the subjects and is equally in all their minds. But although this is a distanced narrator it's certainly not an objective one. This narrator makes judgements on the characters, and uses loaded language so that, paradoxically, this omniscient narrator takes on a highly personal character.

This narrator has a very pronounced attitude towards these characters. Yet this attitude doesn't need to be spelled out. Exactly where is the attitude coming out in each sentence? Have a look at the adjectives and adverbs, and see how different the point of view is when some are removed:

> After several years of childbirth, Mrs Hare had succeeded in having this little girl. They named her Mary, because the mother was too exhausted to think and the father, who would have plunged with excitement into the classics, or the works of Tennyson, to dredge up some name for a son, turned his back on the prospect of a daughter. So Mary the latter became, but a Protestant one.
>
> Mrs Hare had soon taken refuge from Mary in a kindness, with which she continued to deal her a series of blows during what passed for childhood...

Now the verbs are carrying the work of establishing the attitude: here's how it looks with some of the more vivid verbs gone or weakened:

> After several years of childbirth, Mrs Hare had this little girl. They named her Mary, because the mother was too exhausted to think and the father, who would have looked up the classics, or the works of Tennyson, to find some name for a son, turned his back on the prospect of

a daughter. So Mary the latter became, but a Protestant one . . .

In an example like this, point of view isn't explicit in what's said, but in individual words that carry a strong emotional weight.

• • •

And Granma said 'You are the descendant of an Irish race of kings'. You must remember it when you didn't fancy the white of your egg, when it was Betsy Brown pudding for tea; when Mama looked worse and it was your fault: wasting disease they called it and, at the last, foam came out of her mouth, the doctor looked weary as he wiped it away. And Papa was a wild man, crying; he was only a child, younger than you — throwing himself on the bed, grasping her cold hand. But he hated you. It was you who did it — killed her. You were too big as a baby, Boy O'Brien. Coming out, you tore her; you rent her private places.

• From *The Frangipani Gardens*,
Barbara Hanrahan, p. 3.

Having established the basic mood of second person in this first paragraph of the novel, the narrative broadens out a page or two later, so that the same person is both 'you' and 'he':

In the beginning they weren't Girlie and Boy. She was Kathleen, he was Pat; it was Adelaide, but they owned proper Irish names, bestowed with a holy water sprinkle. But Mama died and then Mass stopped — you weren't anything then.

Girlie always wheedled a cuddle. She was older than Boy, but she was treated as little sister. She was a drawing room charmer, dimpled and lisping, but when she had you alone she'd pinch, and: Do this, she'd say, do that. Or she'd start off on her mocking silvery laugh, and the thing that meant most lost its flavour. What did he want with those seed packets? It was unnatural . . . constantly fiddling with them — a great boy like that.

He grew careful. Nothing should betray him again. He kept away from the florist's shop with its moist secret smells. Feeling made you vulnerable, so Boy gave it up. Courage, lad. As you strengthen the body, so will the mind become strong. Go in for games, take lots of exercise and a cold bath each morning. You will live to laugh at your fears yet.

He turned into a scholar, someone who lived through his mind. He had an athlete's body, he used the dumb bells daily, but he didn't see the strong brown limbs or the boxer's chest. A mind was the main thing, Boy's was wonderfully rational. The lovely finality of history—all those dates that heralded all those countless endings—was what he liked best. Dates and death and war—that was history for Boy. The true heir by blood. Direct and perpetual antagonists. Mortal wounds, treasonous intrigues... history was real.

• *The Frangipani Gardens*, pp. 4–5.

Now it becomes clear that this odd stance is perfect for this particular character, who is seeking to distance himself from himself.

Exercises

T HE point of view we think in is first person—our own
perceptions and our own words—so we'll start there.

4.1 Write a portrait of yourself—your physical appearance
and your personality—from your point of view, in the
first person.

It will have a fairly limited point of view, as you don't
know the 'objective' truth about yourself, you only know
what you think. It's likely to have a kind of intimacy,
although it might be critical as well as sympathetic. See
what you discover when you do this:

4.2 Using the same basic facts and information, re-write
this portrait from the point of view of one of your
parents.

The subject of the portrait, yourself, will now be a third
person in the writing. The parent narrating will know different kinds of things and might have different judgements.
They might conceal and reveal different things and for
different reasons. They have a vested interest here, too:
they are connected to the person they're describing and
might feel ashamed, proud, responsible, guilty or self-
satisfied. There might be some distance on the subject: this
time the intimacy may be with the parent doing the narrating.
Now let's take a step further away again.

4.3 Re-write the description from the point of view of
someone writing your biography, a hundred years in
the future. This person may have access to all the
above information, plus some more, and on the other
hand may not know certain things.

This will be a third-person account. There may be no limitations to knowledge, and although there may still be judgements, the narrator won't have a personal stake in the description. The subject will be seen at a great distance and in an impersonal way; the subject will be seen to be just one individual among many, and all affected by the mood and theories of the times.

These narrators are all trying to tell the truth as they see it. But let's explore the murky depths of untruth.

No one ever says anything bad in an obituary. This usually means that the whole truth is not usually being told. Sometimes an obituary is just one long gush. A more interesting obituary is where the person giving it never actually says anything bad about the dead person, but you get the picture just the same. The pleasure is in reading between the lines.

4.4 Write a portrait of yourself, in the third person, using the same basic facts, in the form of an obituary.

4.5 Now we'll try the other end of the spectrum: write the portrait of yourself from the point of view of your worst enemy. It should still sound like the truth, but it will be slanted to bias the reader against you.

Have a look now at all these versions of the same basic material. Which one did you find most interesting to write or read? Which was funniest? Which was most enigmatic? Which was most dramatic? Did any of them suggest stories within stories, layers of meanings?

Once you've written a piece, in whatever point of view came naturally, you can ask yourself what other points of view are possible for the material and which one might work best. Some more than others will offer potential for suspense, drama, pathos, humour or polemic.

4.6 Write a summary of the Cinderella story from the point of view of Cinderella.

Think about what a different story it would be if it was written from another point of view. For example, you could re-tell it from the point of view of another character in the story: the Prince, the Fairy Godmother, the Ugly Sisters, the Step-mother.

You could re-tell it from the point of view of someone with personal interest in the story; someone with a step-mother they dislike or someone who does housework all day or a plain woman who happens to have a beautiful step-sister.

You could tell it from the point of view of someone with a specialised interest or expertise in some feature of the story: a shoe-fetishist, an expert on fairytales, a private detective, a vegetable grower.

You could re-tell the story from the point of view of an all-knowing narrator who could look into the hearts of all the characters.

4.7   Re-tell the story from another point of view, or several.

Which version did you most enjoy writing? Which one flowed most easily? Which one made you think of other things you could write about? Which had most feeling?

Building your story

F IRST, go through all the exercises you've done for this chapter and make a note of anything in them that you might be able to use, or just things that you found interesting to write. It might be just an idea — the idea of an obituary, for example. It might be a new character that appeared as you wrote the exercises. There could be a sentence you like for some reason, a phrase — even a single word that you were pleased to find on the page. Add them all, just as notes, to your piles.

Now think about the point of view of your story. You have two basic choices. Your story can be told from the point of view of someone in the story, or from a point of view outside the story. Consider these two possibilities separately.

Go back to the list of characters that you made in the last chapter. One by one, consider them as candidates for the story-telling role. The most straight forward way would be to discover the story through the eyes of one of the main characters. However, a minor character might provide a more interesting, less obvious way of telling the story. A minor character might be in a position to know or guess things that a major character can't. On the other hand, a minor character mightn't know things and that could be more dramatic, or ironic. Some characters will probably have a more interesting 'voice' than others, or one that you find more natural to write. Some characters might want to persuade the reader of something, while others might be fairly neutral, and either could provide a good point of view.

At this point you're probably not too sure about those events. The story is only an embryo and you may not know what it's about or what happens in the plot. For the moment, don't worry about that.

Rather than thinking in terms of plot-line, think in terms of junctions in your draft: some point in your draft where two different currents meet. For example, points where two characters interact or a character interacts with a significant object.

Take each of your characters in turn and write a paragraph or so from their point of view, either in the first person or subjective third-person. Free-associate: the aim here is to feel the limitations or advantages of telling the story through this character, not to worry about what actually happens in the story.

Now consider the other way of telling the story; from the point of view of a God-like narrator standing outside the events. Take a scene from the story and write it from the point of view of an all-seeing, all-knowing, uninvolved story-teller.

Now assess what you've discovered from all this. Ask the same questions you did about the Cinderella exercise: which one was easiest (or least hard) to write? Which one has possibilities for humour or irony? Which one was most surprising and least obvious? Keep in mind those basic questions: who is telling this story, how much do they know, are they telling the truth.

By the time you've worked through the next few chapters, you may find this will change. Point of view, even more than other areas of writing, is all about trial and error. Sometimes the point of view of a story is there from the beginning and never changes. Very often, though, you might try several different versions.

As you write those different versions, the language will change. Different points of view will express themselves in different word choice and sentence construction. Different points of view will emphasise different things: there'll be detailed descriptions of certain things and only a passing reference to others. Some versions will involve dialogue, and the events might be told in a different order, depending on who's telling the story.

That's what the next chapter concentrates on: finding the right voice for whoever it is telling your story.

5. Voice

You can't have a story without a voice. As soon as you use words, you're making a series of decisions about how you'll put them together, and those decisions reflect the writer's subjective judgement as to which words sound best. You can't have a piece of writing without that subjective element, so there can't be any such thing as a completely neutral voice in fiction.

Voice could also be called 'style': but style sounds like a polish applied at the end whereas voice is an integral part of the whole story. Voice isn't just a few tricks of language but part of the texture of the story.

Good style

You sometimes hear about something called 'good style', but my own view is that there's no such thing. Rather than asking whether a style is correct or incorrect, good or bad, it's more useful to a writer to ask: is this the best style *for this particular story*? Does it enhance what I'm trying to do in the story, or work against it? Every story has its own voice, just as every person does.

Just because you're writing rather than speaking, you don't have to adopt a special literary way of using language. This is fiction, not essay writing: you can break the rules of grammar and 'good English' if it helps the story.

Voice and point of view

The point of view and the voice of a story often match; for example, the voice of 'Reasons for Going into Gynae- cology' is one that we find convincing for a gynaecologist. This is especially true of writing in which the narrator is a character in the story. But it can be intriguing when the point of view and the voice don't match. Imagine the voice of 'Reasons for Going into Gynaecology' telling the story of the bloke on the beach with his binoculars. Imagine the binocular-bloke's story told in the voice of the gynaecologist. It might not 'sound right' but on the other hand it might have the energy and drama of the unexpected, and it might add another, surprising element to the character.

Even when the narrator isn't a character, the voice makes all the difference to the writing. Have another look at the example from Patrick White in the previous chapter and the way the voice changed when adjectives and adverbs were removed.

There are no rights and wrongs with voice. It's very much a matter of intuition which voice sounds right for a particu- lar story. But the more voices you have access to, the greater your range as a writer.

Your own voice and borrowed voices

The voice of a story can be the natural voice of the writer. That natural voice has inbuilt strengths — it usually flows easily, it's consistent, it has the energy of real life and it sounds convincing. Trying to speak with a voice that's not your own is less easy. It's an imitation of a voice rather than a spontaneous one, so there's a danger that it will become lifeless and sound false.

But the decision you make about point of view might mean that you have to contrive a voice that's appropriate for the point of view, which might not be your own voice. So the challenge for a writer is to find a way of keeping the energy and authenticity of your own voice, while adapting it to meet the needs of different points of view.

Before you can adapt your own voice, you have to be able to recognise it. Your own voice is a kind of home base, from which you make explorations out into other voices. The better you know your own voice, the more controlled those explorations will be and the better they're likely to work.

Each of us possesses a voice that's uniquely our own, but we're not always encouraged to value that voice. Because we spend so much time learning 'correct' English and studying 'great' writing, it's easy to feel that our own ungrammatical and uninspired voice isn't good enough. So there's a temptation, especially when writing, to borrow a voice that we feel is more acceptable. After the borrowing has gone on for a while, it becomes automatic and it becomes harder to hear the natural voice beneath the layers of borrowings.

A writer's first task is to encourage that natural voice to be heard. It may not be a 'correct' voice and it may not sound like 'good writing'. But it has something that the most correct and literary voice may not have — it's unique. Yours is an individual voice because you're an individual, not quite like any other. Whatever good things come out of your writing will happen because of that individuality — the fact that no two humans are exactly the same.

In listening for your own voice, you become more sensitive to the different voices you're borrowing. That lets you use them in a controlled way, when you need to, instead of having them dominate your writing.

'Keep it simple, keep it clear'

Very plain prose is often praised for being 'crisp' and 'economical'. These are good qualities and make writing easy to read. However, highly wrought, elaborate prose can be exhilarating. See the example from Campbell on pp. 87–88 or Hazzard on pp. 5–6. Writing should be comprehensible but clarity is not the only virtue in fiction.

What's thought of as 'good writing' often makes use of figures of speech — metaphors, similes, personification and so on. These devices can make a piece of writing sparkle, but if they're used too heavily or inappropriately, they clog it. They're not necessary to make a piece of writing interesting — if in doubt, leave them out.

Cliché

Clichés are words or expressions that roll easily off the tongue: common ways of expressing an idea. When they were first used they were vivid and fresh, but even the best ideas go stale when they become too familiar.

Clichés come in all areas of writing: in ideas, in plot, in characters and most especially in language. Most of us find ourselves writing in clichés from time to time. It's fine for a first draft: it's better to write in clichés than not to write at all. In later drafts, though, it's important to read through with cliché–detectors turned on. It might be appropriate for the voice of your narrator to use clichés, for example, Coombs on pp. 111–112 or Moorhead on pp. 118–120. But you need to be able to recognise clichés so that you only use them after making a conscious decision that they're right for the story.

Sometimes, though, this concern about clichés can lead to the opposite problem: straining after an original or arresting phrase in every single sentence. This can make the writing sound very laboured and contrived.

What is voice?

Many things go together to make up a voice, among them:
- word choice
- syntax
- imagery and figures of speech
- punctuation
- dialogue.

We'll look at all these factors in relation to particular pieces of writing.

Examples

IT'D be a roasting hot summer's arvo and dad'd suddenly knock off hosing down the fence, his eyes'd light up like a railway station cordial machine and he'd utter those words of joy to the family... *'To the beach then, eh?'*

We'd grab our grandmothers and togs and be at the front gate, all sporting Coles' sunglasses and beachball puncture kits, corktipped badminton bats, fruitcake tins and nose-lotion. Not having a car, we'd fry on the Reservoir station, our teeth totally into Choc Wedges, waiting for that heavenly VicRail chariot, whose driver was always Paul Robeson, to sail us away to such Troppo-madness ports of call as Aspendale, St Kilda and Chelsea.

I'll never forget waiting for the beach-train. Through the heatshimmer of skinheads, bodgies, spat-out Kool Mint and KitKat, the tracks baked along with the signals and maggies croaking as one.

Dad cursed the cars rattling down High Street with their roofracks brimming with Super-Pal Kickboards. 'I oughta get a bloody licence, love,' he'd say, but mum'd hold his hand and unpeel a Mintie for him knowingly. We were happy in those days. Mum always knew best.

Dis Train Am Bound For Glory Dis Train would finally snore into the station and we'd hop on. Louts would entertain the sweltering passengers. It was an eternity, but somehow we always got there, and then dad'd have to buy more tickets at Flinders Street station to go on to the beach.

Huge mobs of Orange-Fanta ockers queueing up for beach tickets, some families a wonderful primrose, others the same pink as spout-primer, others scarlet vermilion, picked out in pumpkin-yellow towel and chocolate thong.

The conversation'd go a bit like this. 'Two and six halves return to Bonbeach and a pensioner. Here, there's a quid there. What? Of course she's old! Of course she's a pensioner! Go on mum, tell 'em how old you are! Look she's got a card, isn't that enough for you.' Then mum'd say, 'Grab the change, love, nothing ya can do about it. Come on let's get away for that nice swim, eh? Here, Darl, have another Mintie and cheer up a bit.'

That cool effervescent hit of sea salt air wafting up our swollen sinuses, working its way through our Capstan-coated lungs. We'd stroll around the neighbouring shops in a dream, mum looking at bras and dad looking at guns.

    • From 'To the Beach Then, eh?', Barry Dickins, from
The Gift of the Gab, pp. 27–28.

This piece of writing sounds like a speaking voice. That's not to say it just came out like that first time — it might have taken weeks to achieve this tone of artless informality. But the result is a voice that you can hear very clearly, that sounds very 'real': the writer is borrowing the energy of real speech.

What makes this voice sound the way it does?

Look at the word-choice — 'arvo' instead of 'afternoon', but also 'utter' rather than 'say'. What do those lists of brand names and place names do? Look at the verbs and imagine the piece with less dynamic ones.

Look at the syntax: the length and complexity of the sentences in the first four paragraphs, and then the two very short, simple ones at the end of that paragraph, for example. Look at the way things are put together un-expectedly — 'we'd grab our grandmothers and togs'.

Look at the figures of speech: a simile like 'his eyes'd light up like a railway station cordial machine' tells us as much about the narrator as it does about Dad's eyes, and so does the imagery about the colours further on. The other kind of imagery is the opposite; not everyday but grandiose — 'that heavenly VicRail chariot . . . ' What does that do?

Look at the punctuation: Dickins has only used commas and full stops, and many contractions, some of them not ones you normally see written down.

Look at the dialogue: does it sound real to you? Why?

Voice alone can tell us a lot about the narrator. In this example, we could be fairly confident that the narrator isn't the headmaster of Geelong Grammar or a bishop. How do we know? We've got some ideas about what this narrator *isn't,* so can we draw a portrait of what he or she *is,* just from the way the words are put together here?

•••

In the morning the father throws the dog in the water. The dog paddles madly to the shore. The father talks about snags in the river. They all discuss the difference between snags as in water hazards and snags as in sausages. Sausage dogs. Smoke. Children who've drowned. Bushfires. Snakes. Carpet snakes. The long grass. The blackberry patch. The tar baby. Was there such a thing as Brer Bear. The pyjama girl. Bullrushes. Flash floods. Flying foxes. The hazards of flying foxes. High tensile wires and electricity lines. Broken electricity lines hanging down into creeks. Fords with cars on them washed away in flash floods. River snakes. March flies. Bot flies. The difference between bot flies and sand flies. Maggots in sausages. Maggot stories. Meat safe stories. Ice chest stories. Milk delivery when milk was in buckets. The bread cart. The sound of the bread cart. Draught horses. Old draught horses. Horses being sent off to the blood and bone factory. Horses in the city. Sewerage. The sewerage works. Polluted creeks. The correct drinking sections of the creeks. The aeration process. Stagnant water. Boiling the billy. Billy tea. The Billy Tea brand name. The inferior quality of Billy Tea. Swaggies. Gypsies. The cleverness of gypsies. Poverty. Bread and dripping. Sausages. Home-grown vegetables. Outdoor toilets. Improvised toilet paper. The long summer nights. Mosquitoes. Marshes and bogs. Moonee Moonee and Brooklyn. The possibility of a mosquito breeding in the dew on a leaf. Bites. Bee stings. Allergies to bites. Death from bee stings. How to make a whistle from a leaf. Playing the comb. The mouth harp. The bush bass. Bottle tops. The corrosive qualities of Coca Cola. Big Business. Monopolies. Bigger and bigger monopolies. Free enterprise. Russia. The idea of women working in men's jobs. Suez. American election campaigns. The Ku Klux Klan. The colour bar. The Iron Curtain. The Cold War. The ideals of communism as distinct from the practice. China. Industrialisation. Cuba. Atheism and agnosticism. The idea of the supreme being. The church in Russia. The Jews. Israel. The world wars. The next one. The fatalistic approach. The end of civilisation. The end of the human race. The inexorable continuation of the universe in spite of the human race. Humans as microscopic and trivial beings. The frailty of humans. The stupidity of humans. The innate badness of humans. Animal life and animals' code of behaviour. The rationality of animals. The fowls of the air and other biblical quotes. And now I see as through a glass darkly.

At the end of the last hand of 500, they remember other discussions they've had and that they always concluded with politics. The father turns down the Tilley lamp.

> • From 'Xmas in the Bush', Anna Couani, in
> *Transgressions*, p. 191.

Dickins takes the odd liberty with grammar and has a list or two, but in this piece Anna Couani takes that loose use of language much further. This extract is a sort of story-as-free-association. Do you find it funny? Why?

• • •

... and here is a little packet of Strasbourg sausages ... the production line must be amazing: endless tube of pale pink emulsified meat, as homogenized as bland as a cherub's cheek, sliding through some vacuum machine into the long column of red skin and then there must be some kind of twisting device to divide the infinite sausage, another to slap them side to side, pushing out the air, shrinking the plastic pack around, so snug around these neat little jobs: toy phallic food of a ludic psycho-critic. In the trolley is the plastic litre of *Grand Margnat*, three francs fifty, green lentils, two francs forty, pale food of denial that one flavours over hours with this and that; will try it, have a holiday from the rich animal fat, eat it as floury air food for Laurence, her palate so discerning that the faintest taste becomes a wealth and now ... hand is on the little round-contoured block of mini-sausages; for fun, against the lentils, will dine on that, and so very cheap, somehow the pack is so graspable, it is graspable, the hand is slipping into this pocket not into the trolley, I have done it *I have done it* and as I reach for the milk, suddenly the left hand is the only one available, trolley glides its reflection over the mock-marble vinyl tiles the gloss the gloss of it, smiling, again

at the *fromagière*, this is the treacherous smile now, there is no stitching in that pocket, bottomless . . . hand must suspend the sausages against the leg and sausages strung on air, approaching the check-out desk now . . *This, my dear is the real thing,* she quips, genuine R.A.F., a flyer's coat Rita Rita Aviator. This right sleeve is joined now to the pocket, fingers married to the little pink stubbies dangling in the void . . . MADEMOISELLE *venez par ici, s'il vous plaît* . . . and what is the moustached giant in the dark blue suit doing here now? Up there the little office with its glass walls is . . . its door is open: he has descended from his elevated aquarium to invite me to another cash-desk and yet, why this privilege? At the one I have chosen there is no great queue. Now with the left hand, must do some tricky steering of the trolley, the wheels have a will of their own, how to pay for the wine, milk, lentils with this left hand? The purse won't obey, stud will not give way under thumb . . . does it look feasible to keep one hand casually pocketed while struggling with the other one to unload the goods from the trolley and pay up? MADEMOISELLE, *voulez-vous bien retirer votre main de votre poche?* Hand from pocket, he wants the hand from the pocket . . . the words making another, fish-bowl around me . . . no a gossamer globe rather and what a relief in the take-off up up up going up, people heaping up behind me, *ces mères de familles, je sais voler, on m'appelle voleur* . . . the coat is separating me, darkness severs from the gloss of it all and I was wrong, they are so red, not pink, so nude, on the cash-desk, the *saucisses de Strasbourg 'VENEZ PAR ICI MADEMOISELLE'*. When you buy you are *Madame,* when you steal you are *Mademoiselle* up up we go together, dark dark blue with the dark dark blue to the glassy observation booth where, why . . . yes, of course, he has seen it all.
• From *Lines of Flight*, Marion Campbell, pp. 41–42.

Voice in fiction can be like a speaking voice, but it can also be the voice of the mind: 'stream-of-consciousness'. The voice of this extract conveys the reader directly into the mind of a woman in a supermarket in France. The first-person point of view already tends to make the reader identify with the narrator, and the voice deepens this effect.

We seem to be right in this woman's mind, hearing her thoughts as she has them, not arranged into neat grammatical sentences. Notice the way words are used: phrases and words are repeated, also the way articles and pronouns are left out at times in a sort of hasty shorthand. Things are not explained for the reader but are simply presented.

Notice also the syntax and punctuation: thoughts are not always arranged into sentences but simply flow from one to the next, and yet it's not hard to follow. The Dickins example used conventional grammar, and only needed commas and full stops. The Couani example abandoned grammar but used only very short, one-thought sentences. In this example, when it suits the pace of the action, Campbell abandons grammar in favour of an accelerating flow of thoughts. When a writer chooses to do this, the danger is that the writing can become hard to follow. Campbell has ensured against this by making maximum use of that other clarifying device — punctuation. Punctuation becomes important as an aid to tone of voice and comprehension when you're not using conventional syntax. In this example, Campbell has made use of almost every kind of punctuation, and used different type-faces as well in order to make sure the reader continues to hear a voice that can be clearly heard and understood.

Notice the imagery and the figures of speech: as well as individual imagery — the cherub, the fish bowl — Campbell has incorporated a larger image into this scene. One of the recurring metaphors in this book is the image of flight, and the double meanings involved in this word in both French and English. In French, the pun is between flying and stealing. How appropriate, then, that the treacherous flyer's jacket is the mechanism for the action in this scene.

Notice the dialogue. What is the effect of using italics for the dialogue, rather than the conventional method of quotation marks and a separate line?

•••

After it was all over, after the sleeping children were carried through the night to their beds, after the closest neighbours had set off in their traps in the moonlight, after the maids had flitted amongst the litter on the lawn, after the dogs had crept up for the bones, after the torches had been extinguished — after it was all over,

Niall lay in one of Goonda's many beds in one of
Goonda's many guest-rooms and dreamt of women,
masses of them, thousands of them, crowds of them all
dressed in huge sun-hats, each carrying a parasol,
moving and milling in plazas and squares, rising and
dropping on a lacework of stairways, standing and sitting on platforms and balconies and towers and gaze-
bos, and from the centre of them all, from the very
centre of the focus of their collective attention, there rose
a statue, a heavy monument achingly solid which nevertheless rose, seemed to levitate, stood in the air, plinth
and all, a statue of the Empire's Queen gripping all the
instruments of her office, the mace, the sceptre, the
crown, with at her feet the lion of Africa, the tiger of
India, the wild dog of Australia, while beneath it all,
straining on the wires keeping the statue aloft, were
Niall and two other men whose bulging throats gave out
a triad howl, a chord of desperation, pumped from
strangling muscles and knotted tendons, so that Niall
awoke with the howl still quivering in the moonlight in
the room and he wondered, fearing, whether others in
the house had heard him call out. But he need not have
worried, for the howl came again, staining the air in the
hot room, tearing and dripping along the moonlight in
hot gouts of sound. It was the implacable howl of the
creature outside the window, the dingo pacing the narrow perimeter of the cage, ablaze with moonlight, stopping again to ululate for the wild, fecund horizon
beyond the cage bars.
- From *Matilda My Darling*, Nigel Krauth, p. 124.

The previous examples all sounded like speaking voices
of different kinds. But the voice of a piece of writing, such
as this one, can be very 'literary' and not like a spoken voice
at all. In this example, look at the structure of the extremely
long first sentence. To see how its machinery works, try
stripping it of all its repetitions and elaborations, or imagine
it cut up into a number of short sentences. The unstoppable,
accelerating horror of a nightmare is perfectly reflected in
the long, single sentence in a way that would be weakened
by another choice of syntax.

The language is formal and studied, with many words not

found in everyday usage—words such as levitate, triad, implacable, fecund aren't usually found in speech, for example, or newspaper writing.

•••

The piles of debris were fresh, some smouldering. He could see the men amongst the tall timber from a distance. Some were cutting high on trees, others clearing the brush. Back towards the tents two bullock teams were lined parallel, a dozen in each to pull the larger timber from the bush. Men were up on a length that had been felled. They were removing all the branches from its top side, throwing them to the ground. There, groups of people collected and piled it, women and men. Blacks in clothes. Aboriginal children too. All gathering it up in their arms and pulling the larger pieces and throwing it all into a series of piles.

The man highest on one tree had finished and started down, removing his stands as he descended. When he reached the ground those around him became hurried. They took their handfuls quickly to the piles and gathered together. The black children, some who couldn't have reached their third birthdays, took hold of a mother's leg or grabbed each other. Some placed their tiny hands over their ears and put their heads down. Then the men around the feller moved back and he put the final cuts in. The tree seemed to teeter up high as if it would stay. The feller, and others around the site whose trees were not so far gone, watched that apex. The leaves moved slowly from side to side, as if in some transient wind. It became unsteady in fractions.

It would fall on the workers. He was sure. But none of them moved, confident in the feller's skill. It leant further one way, unable to hold itself. The crack was from its heart. The heartwood was torn and the huge base bounced up and off the stump, branches of other trees and shrubs were broken and thrown into the air.

No shouts went up. It was commonplace. Before the tree settled the workers had moved in. A man close by, in a hat misshapen by being too long in the wet, yelled something incomprehensible at the bullocks. His whip sounded out as if it had broken. The beasts at the front pushed their hooves in and shouldered forward. Then the whip lashed out again and they all seemed to move at once. It was slow movement and the chains behind barely sounded. Then again. And they moved as one. The driver's voice grunted commands. They moved towards the fallen log, making the chains clink. Some men were up on the log. Others were on the ground. One on the bottom of the saw, one on the top-handle. Each pair would saw until they'd reached their limit. All three could be working, sometimes none. The sliding, scraping sound surged through the bush.

Sidney sketched quickly, making notes on the side of each sheet. There were muted colours, pale lemon, and lilac, cast by the smoke of the debris high in the branches. The shirts of the men, some checked, some plain, blended uneasily into the bush. In places where a hole had been made in a canopy the workers were highlighted.

- From *Black Cat, Green Field*, Graeme Harper, p. 107.

This example is also not like a spoken voice, in spite of the simplicity of the style. Try reading it aloud to feel where it differs from a spoken voice. The strength comes from the repetition of simple syntax and simple words. There's a quality of reduction about it, and in fact some sentences have been reduced down to a single phrase. Partly for these reasons, the emphasis is on the senses: what can be seen and heard, rather than on thoughts or judgements. This is appropriate, as the main character is a painter.

Exercises

L IKE point of view, the voice of a story might come naturally in the first draft and never need changing. But you might also find, as you explore a story, that you need to re-think the voice completely. Point of view and voice are bound up very closely because the voice belongs to the narrator whose point of view we're hearing. If you change one, you're likely to need to change the other.

The voice that comes most naturally to you is your own, so we'll start with that.

5.1 Think of some example of minor conflict that you've been involved with in the last week with a member of your family or friend. Write a short account of it as if for a diary you're keeping: you're writing it just for your own interest and you're the only reader.

The readership of this was you alone, so you weren't thinking about its effect on anyone else. You might have mentioned things that mean something only to you, and you might have used shorthand words that only you understand.

As soon as you start thinking about someone else reading it, you'd want to change things: not so much in the events described, as in the way you've described them. You might need to explain things more and you might want to make sure that your reader feels the same way you did about the incident.

5.2 Write the incident again but this time write it as a letter to a friend (not the one you're having the conflict with).

The voice is still yours but the writing has changed to take account of the reader. You have to be clearer and you might have to explain things: above all, you need to make sure that the reader sees the conflict the same way you do. You'll be choosing your words for their effect on the reader. The reader is a particular individual: the words you choose will be affected by what you know of that individual, too. Notice where you've made changes and what sort of changes they are.

5.3 Now re-write this letter: this time it's being written as evidence in a court of law.

This account will be very sober, unemotional and more formal. It's still your voice but it's your voice at its most controlled. The readership now is not an individual known to you, but an unknown number of unknown readers. Let's now try borrowing someone else's voice.

5.4 Imagine you are that person you've been in conflict with. In that other person's voice, write a letter about the conflict. The letter is addressed to you: this letter will be the mirror-image of the one in exercise 5.2.

Now you're looking at the incident from the other person's point of view and you'll also be using their voice. As well as interpreting the events differently, this other person will choose different ways of expressing themselves.

Think about how that person uses language: do they use the same sort of vocabulary you do? Do they talk more formally, or less? Are they more articulate than you, or less? Do they use a lot more unfinished sentences or exclamations than you do? Do they say straight out what they mean or do you have to read between the lines? Are they ironic? Do they express themselves in cool, rational ways or are they highly emotional?

So far, all these voices have been versions of real ones. Now let's use these real voices as a basis for a fictional one.

5.5 Take the last exercise and list the characteristics of the voice. Go through, one by one, the areas of word use, syntax, imagery, punctuation and dialogue, and describe this voice.

Now re-write the paragraph, exaggerating those qualities. Don't worry about going too far—this is only an exercise. Make the word use ridiculously colloquial or ridiculously formal; make the syntax absurdly long-winded or incredibly terse, and so on.

You might never have tried writing in such extreme ways before—you might find that it broadens your own range of voice.

The voice of a piece of writing can tell us a lot about the narrator: think of the Dickins example on p. 84. Take the exercise you've just done and see how much information about the narrator you can convey just in the voice. Don't worry about it being any real person: this is fiction now. And if you need to make the voice less extreme, do so. One by one, think about those elements of syntax, word use, punctuation and dialogue, and see if you can make each of them do some work in telling us something about the narrator.

These exercises are based on a narrator who's a character in the story. Many of the same ideas apply even when the narrator isn't a character in the story. Look again at the examples by Krauth and Harper (pp. 89–90 and 91–92). These narrators aren't characters, but the voice they choose adds to the force of the writing. In order to see what they add, it might be useful to look at the same subject matter expressed in a different voice. See what happens when you try this.

5.6 Take the first sentence of the Krauth example and re-write it in the voice of the Harper example. This will mean cutting it up into many short sentences, emphasising visual qualities rather than abstract ones, using very plain words, and so on. Then take the first paragraph of the Harper example and re-write it in the voice of the Krauth example. The sentences will be joined up to make longer, complex ones, there will be more adjectives and adverbs, more abstractions, more high-flown words, etc.

You might feel the piece has gained something by the change, or lost, or simply feels different. Try to pinpoint just what it is that's changed.

Paradoxically, copying the voice of another writer is a very good way to learn something about your own voice and to encourage it to broaden its possibilities.

5.7 Take the Krauth example, or the Harper example, or any other piece of writing where the narrator isn't a character in the fiction. Re-write your piece about conflict, copying the voice of the piece you've chosen.

Building your story

F IRST, look through all the exercises you've just done and copy anything you think you might be able to use in your embryonic story. It doesn't have to be much: a single word or a phrase is worth keeping, or an event or a feeling that might be useful in your story.

From the exercises in Chapter 4, you probably have some idea now which point of view is likely to be a promising one for this story. Perhaps you have a couple of possible points of view. The task now is to explore the most interesting voice for that point of view.

From Chapter 4, take a piece that you've written in the point of view you think you might use. Make two lists.

1 What the voice is like. Make a note of word use, syntax, whether the voice is formal or chatty, etc.
2 What the narrator is like. If this narrator is a character in the story, make a note of the things about them that might make a difference to their voice: their age, their background, their education, their attitude to the events, and so on. If the narrator isn't a character in the story, think about whether you want their voice to convey an obvious attitude to the events, or whether it should be more impartial.

Compare your lists. They might match up well; for example, the voice might be very chatty and informal and the narrator might be the man who runs the corner shop. They might not match so well in other ways: the voice might be youthful slang but the narrator is sixty years old. The ways they don't match might be more interesting than the ways they do match and might suggest new possibilities about character. You may see elements in the second list that you can add to the first so that the voice tells us more about the narrator. You may see places where the voice is too much your own voice and not enough the voice of the narrator. You might see places where the voice just 'feels wrong'. There might be nothing wrong with the voice but it might be rather bland and uninteresting.

Transform this piece by trying these exercises, keeping in the back of your mind the point of view that this voice is expressing.

> Have a look at list one: what the voice is like. One by one, make all the characteristics of your piece into their opposites. If your piece has very plain language, make it as elaborate as you can. If the syntax is very simple, write long convoluted sentences. If there's no imagery, load it with metaphors and similes. If there are only commas and full stops, try using all the other kinds of punctuation. If there's direct speech, make it indirect.
>
> Have a look at list two: what the narrator is like. If your narrator is a character in the story, try writing the piece so that the voice tells us as much as possible about the narrator. Try to think of a model for the character from real life—a person, or several people, whose qualities you can draw on for your character, and think of their voices. As you did in the exercises, work through the different elements of syntax, choice of words, and so on, and make each one convey something about the narrator. If your narrator isn't a character in the story, you can still try different voices. Is this narrator very dead-pan about the events or very emotional? Does the narrator just describe what can be seen and heard? Or does the narrator speculate, judge, approve or disapprove, go into abstractions or generalisations? Have a look at the examples of narrators in Murnane pp. 6–7, Hazzard pp. 5–6, Jolley pp. 44–45, White pp. 71–72, Harrower pp. 109–111, Coombs pp. 111–112 and Garner pp. 107–109 for some idea of the range of narrative voices that's possible. Try re-writing your narrative voice in as many different kinds of voices as you can. A paragraph or two will be enough to see whether it's working.

Some of these voices will seem obviously wrong but some that you might have thought would sound wrong might work surprisingly well. Those surprises might lead you to re-think the narrator entirely. You could go back to your list of possible points of view for the story from the previous chapter and try them all with their different voices. It might be that a point of view which you didn't think would work goes with an interesting voice, so you might decide to go with that point of view after all.

There are certain discoveries that you can only make by actually trying things out on paper, even if they seem unpromising. These surprises are what will save the writing from being flat and unexciting. As you experiment with different voices, the writing will suddenly take on depth and colouring as if a sound-track has been added: the writing will start to live through its voice.

Now, rather than starting with a character and adding a voice, try the opposite.

Think about the people you know. How do they speak? Are there some who have a particular, idiosyncratic way of expressing themselves? Perhaps they always talk full-pelt, the ideas tumbling all over themselves and no thought finished before the next is rushing along. Perhaps they speak with long pauses, groping for the right words. Perhaps they have colourful turns of phrase or a quirky way of saying things. Perhaps they have a habit of irony and say what they mean by saying the opposite.

Think about pieces of writing by other writers, writing that you like. What sort of voices do they have? Do they sound like speaking voices, or are they unmistakably a written use of language? Are they straightforward voices, or do they sometimes disguise their meaning behind humour, or irony, or elaboration?

Imagine your story told through one of these voices and write a paragraph or two this way. It might sound all wrong, in which case you'll have learnt something about what might sound right. On the other hand, it might suggest a whole new way of telling the story. A voice might be a starting point around which you change everything else to fit.

At the end of all these experiments you'll probably have a good idea what voice is most likely to work for your story. At the very least, you'll know which ones sound all wrong.

Go through all the fragments you've got and write them all in the point of view you've decided on and in the voice you think works best.

In doing this, you'll probably find that the fragments are starting to join up in some kind of order because they're now unified by all going through the same channel of voice and point of view. You might change all this completely before the story's finished, but doing it will give rise to new ideas about the story as a whole.

The voice of a story might sound like a speaking voice, or it might not. But as well as the narrative voice, fiction often has literal voices as well, in the form of dialogue. This is what the next chapter will look at.

6  Dialogue

Just as a person is not the same as a character, speech is not the same as dialogue. Dialogue is an artificial construction designed to live on the written page. There's an overlap between speech and dialogue, but they're not the same thing. There's a paradox about dialogue in fiction, which is that in order to achieve the effortless-looking illusion of real speech, the writer has to apply a lot of effort.

Unlike point of view, dialogue in fiction is an optional extra and the options for dialogue are many:

- dialogue can be realistic, or it can be deliberately unnatural and unrealistic
- a story can have no dialogue at all, or it can be virtually all dialogue
- the dialogue can be in the form of direct speech or indirect speech
- dialogue can be conventionally set out on a separate line between quotation marks, or it can blend in with the rest of the text.

Whatever way you want to use dialogue in your fiction, it's useful to start by listening to the characteristics of real speech. If you want to mimic real speech in your dialogue, you'll know what to imitate. And if you want to use dialogue in an unrealistic way, the patterns of real speech will still give you a starting point. What are the characteristics of real speech? From listening closely to almost any real speech, we could list these qualities:

- sentences are sometimes left unfinished

- ideas don't always flow logically, but jump from one thought to another
- it's sometimes ungrammatical
- it needs physical gestures to make the meaning clear
- it's sometimes rambling
- it's sometimes repetitious.

Speech works in real life but it might not work as dialogue on the page. In its written-out form, its problems might be:

- there's no focus, so it's hard to follow
- there are dull parts between the interesting parts
- it assumes knowledge that the reader mightn't have and uses a kind of shorthand
- some of it makes no sense without the gesture or tone of voice or facial expression that went with it.

The purpose of dialogue

Dialogue can be part of a story or it can inspire a story. Since dialogue is an optional extra, if you decide to use it you should ask yourself what purpose it's filling in the story. Here are a few possibilities.

- You might be using dialogue to make the story more like life. Conversations take place in life, so you may wish them to take place in your fiction, too.
- You might be using it to convey character.
- You might be using it to dramatise an incident so that it unfolds before the reader as if in real time.
- You might be using it to get ironic distance on a character.
- You might be using it for a few laughs.

There are some tasks that dialogue should not be called on to do.

- Dialogue is not a good place to convey information. In soap operas, characters often tell other characters things they'd know already, but in a story a writer can convey this kind of information in the narrative.
- Dialogue is not very suitable as a disguise for a philosophical argument.
- Dialogue shouldn't get too bogged down, as real-life speech often does, in dull, mechanical details of daily life.

Dialogue that sounds right

If you choose to use dialogue, you want the reader to hear some version of a speaking voice, even if it's not a realistic one. For that reason, one way to judge whether dialogue is working is to try it out aloud. Best of all is to ask someone else to read it out for you. If you feel that it just doesn't sound right, trust that instinct, even if you don't know why. Dialogue is a kind of music: you have to trust your ear and your instinct.

In life, people do occasionally deliver long speeches, but in a story long speeches don't usually read well. If a character has so much to say, perhaps the story should be written from his or her point of view.

Since speech is usually ungrammatical, dialogue will often sound best if it's ungrammatical, too. But unless you want to draw attention to a character's lack of grammar, you should aim for unobtrusive grammar. A piece of dialogue can often be re-arranged so that it has the loose, unstructured feel of ungrammatical speech without sounding emphatically 'incorrect' or being hard to follow. See for example Helen Garner on pp. 107–109.

Attributions

Attributions are all those 'he said's and 'she saids' in fiction. Attributions are a necessary evil. Too many give a bit of dialogue a monotonous limping feeling. Too few and you lose track of who's saying what. (Although this can, in extremes, be part of the effect: look at the extract from David Foster on pp. 117–118.)

It's tempting to break the monotony with the help of the thesaurus, which has any number of substitutes for 'he said': he can expostulate, moan, whisper, shout, interject and so on, but unless you're writing comedy the thesaurus is not the answer here.

A much more graceful solution is the example from Elizabeth Harrower on pp. 109–111. The pieces of dialogue are separated from each other by small actions or thoughts. These give the reader the clue as to who is speaking. This has the other advantage of providing some of the nonverbal dimension of a conversation: gestures, body language, tone of voice, those pauses between comments.

Sometimes characters have such very different ways of speaking that attribution can be pared right down to the minimum. Each piece of dialogue can contain some tiny piece of information that tells us which character is speaking.

Punctuation

Punctuation is a convenience like musical notation. It's a code for the way a spoken voice should sound reading a piece of writing: where to pause, where to indicate a sidetrack in the thought, which words to emphasise. This applies to narrative as well as dialogue.

It's a code we learn somewhere along the line so we know, for example, that when something's in block letters it's supposed to be shouted. In naturalistic dialogue, punctuation is important because a real spoken voice is being approximated.

Commas are useful to convey that quality of real speech where we string a lot of ideas together loosely in an exploratory way, without giving more weight to one than the other. More emphatic or decisive speech might be a whole string of mini sentences.

Dots and dashes are good — they get across the tentative way speech happens — the thought peters out but the speaker indicates by tone of voice that there's more to follow . . . But too many dots and dashes can get maddening. You want the sentence to come to roost now and again.

Exclamation marks should be used sparingly. Too many make the dialogue sound hysterical. It gets to be exhausting to read. Also, you have nothing up your sleeve when you want to make a really strong point!

Colons and semi-colons tend to be associated with formal, well-considered kinds of writing. You hardly ever see a semi-colon in a newspaper. So in dialogue you have to be aware of that association they have and only use them if that formal tone is what you want.

Best of all is if you can re-arrange the sentence to simplify and minimise punctuation. See what a difference punctuation and gaps makes to this speech from Helen Garner's *The Children's Bach*. This is how it appears in the novel.

> 'They didn't realise for quite a...he never spoke. He does sing. His voice is very...Dexter and his wife thought for a while he was some sort of musical genius. They can be toilet-trained, taught to keep themselves clean...'

This is how it might have looked: correct, but insensitive to the rhythms of real speech:

> 'They didn't realise for quite a while that something was wrong. He never spoke, although he does sing: in fact Dexter and his wife thought for a while he was some sort of musical genius. They can be toilet-trained and taught to keep themselves clean.'

Punctuation will always be only an approximation of the sound of a speech, in the same way that musical notation is only a guide to how a piece of music should sound.

Another factor is whether punctuation should be used to distinguish dialogue from the rest of the text. And, if so, then to what extent. The convention is to start the dialogue on a new line, indent and put each person's speech between double quotation marks. This has the effect of separating the dialogue off very markedly from the narration. In life, dialogue and event and thoughts are all going on simultaneously, so some writers look for other ways of punctuating dialogue that doesn't quarantine it quite so strongly from the rest of the text. Some possibilities are:

- you can use double quotation marks but not start a new line
- you can start a new line but use a dash rather than quotation marks
- you can use no punctuation at all but just run it in with the rest of the narrative.

See the extract from Sue Woolfe on pp. 115–116 for a

successful use of non-standard punctuation, and the extract from Marion Campbell on pp. 87–88.

The only criterion is whether it's clear who's speaking and when they're stopping and starting. It's irritating for a reader not to be sure.

It seems that if you keep dialogue short, you can get away with some of these alternatives. But the conventions of punctuation have evolved because they make writing clear and easy to read, so you should think carefully before abandoning them.

A MAN was sitting with his back to her, just inside the row of plastic potplants which fenced off the cafeteria. She had to narrow herself and slide sideways to get past his inconveniently placed chair. Which of her senses recognised him first? She was close enough to smell his unwashed hair, to see the way his shirt collar stuck up stiffly round his ears, to hear the cheerful slurp of his mouth at the cup. She was right behind him, poised on her toes. Could it be? And if she spoke, would she be sorry afterwards?

'Excuse me,' she said.

He turned his head. It was Dexter.

Oh, her awful modern clothes, her hair spiked and in shock. He saw the fan of lines at the outer corner of her eye and his heart flipped like a fish. He pushed back his chair and stood up in a clumsy rush.

'Morty,' he whispered. 'Morty, look. It's me.'

'I thought it might be,' she said, 'I thought it was.' She heard the warmth go out of her voice and the dryness come in, and wanted to cry for something lost. Why isn't he roaring? Why isn't he making a fuss? Isn't he glad to see me? Don't I look all right? But we never used to hug. Why should we start now?

'You look very—you look—'He could not find a polite word, he was so full of feelings.

'That's the same coat,' she said, stepping back and pointing. 'The same smelly old khaki coat.'

'My father's here,' said Dexter. 'Look, Dad! It's Morty!'

Dexter's father had a paper serviette tucked into his collar and a fork in one hand. He moved his hat off the extra chair and dithered with it. Beside him sat a small boy with pale eyes and a Prince Valiant haircut. Dexter was recovering, was beginning to prance about in his great brogues with his arms out in a curve. Elizabeth slid past him and into the seat.

'I'll go for some cake!' shouted Dexter.

Doctor Fox looked at Elizabeth as he chewed, and

nodded and smiled. She must be nearly forty now, like Dex. Thank God they were never foolish enough to marry, though no doubt Dexter had poked her when they were students. He felt like laughing. She was quite plainly not the marrying kind. Children out of the question. He saw her wide open eyes, her nervous nostrils, her desire to impress, something fancy and successful about her, and yet he felt sure she was the kind of woman who'd throw round terms like *the orthodox feminist position*. He washed down the crumbs with a swig of coffee and waited for her to speak. He guessed what she would say.

She did. 'Isn't Mrs Fox here?'

How sociable. He remembered her at nineteen. She made him an omelette for lunch when his wife was out, a clumsy act of duty, and called him to come and eat it, but he was upstairs nutting out a score and neither answered nor came till the food was cold and flat. She glowered at him from the scullery. The young women liked his wife more than they did him.

'No. My wife's at home. And that's where I'm going.'

His cultivated vowels: mai waife. She longed to whip the serviette out of his collar.

'Is that Dexter's little boy?'

Doctor Fox jumped. 'Yes. One of them. This is William.'

The child had vague eyes. Elizabeth, who was not good with small children, bent across the table and tried to get her face into his line of vision. The boy's gaze drifted, but not towards her. It was like looking at him through water. A smile of blessedness warmed his features and was gone; a little knot of thought bulged between his brows and smoothed itself again. She could not get his attention.

The old man cleared his throat. 'I'm afraid Billy's not quite . . .'

Elizabeth sat up.

'They didn't realise for quite a . . . He never spoke. He does sing. His voice is very . . . Dexter and his wife thought for a while he was some sort of musical genius. They can be toilet-trained, taught to keep themselves clean . . .'

Dexter came charging back. He had one arm above his head, holding a plate with cake on it. He plunged into the seat beside her. 'Shithouse cheese cake,' he roared. He reached across and wedged a piece of it into the little boy's mouth.

• From *The Children's Bach*, Helen Garner, p. 5.

Go through the list of characteristics of real speech on pp. 101–102. How many of them can you find in this extract? Look at how Garner has managed to minimise attributions in different ways, and how the dialogue is interspersed with narrative. If you ran all this dialogue together as one uninterrupted conversation, what would change? Some of the narrative is, in fact, almost dialogue: the character speaking to himself or herself, or imagining dialogue that might take place, so that there's a smooth flow between dialogue and narrative. Notice how very short the pieces of dialogue are, and yet how much information they convey. As in life, a great deal of the conversation is going on in the silences.

• • •

'Now that your father's gone —'

Stella Vaizey saw the two races jerk to an even sharper alertness, and hesitated. What a pair of pedants they were! What sticklers, George Washingtons, optimists!

'Dead,' she corrected herself firmly, with a trace of malice. 'Now that your father's dead, the three of us are going to live together in Sydney.'

The blank receptive faces, the wide-open eyes, turned now to their headmistress, Miss Lambert, who nodded regretful confirmation.

'When I've sold the house and found a flat in the city,' the girls' mother continued, taking in the exchange of looks dryly, 'I'll let Miss Lambert know.'

A magpie or a currawong, or some other bush bird she hoped never to hear in town, gave its careless, beautifully deliberate call from a giant blue gum in the distance outside the school grounds. (Someone sighed.) Closer at hand there were energetic sounds from the tennis courts, and laughter.

'I can't persuade you to reconsider this, Mrs. Vaizey? If we had Laura for her last years — She's one of our best students, you know.' The girl had thought that she might study medicine as her father had done, though

Laura had now and then expressed her willingness, in addition, to sing in opera, if pressed to do so. And laughable and unlikely though such ideas often seemed, it was a fact, Miss Lambert had to admit, that human beings did perform in operas the world over, and that Laura had a charming mezzo-soprano voice, was musical, and had an aptitude for languages. However, her poor young father—at forty-five five years younger than Miss Lambert—had had a heart attack at the wheel of his car setting out one evening to visit a patient; and now, in a sense—from a headmistress's point of view— his daughter's life was in danger. (Clare's too, of course, but she was only nine, not at such a crucial stage; was apt to say, anyway, to benevolent enquiries about her future plans, 'I don't know'—unlike some others of her age, who could already answer, with an aplomb Miss Lambert liked to flatter herself the school had fostered, 'A physiotherapist, Miss Lambert', or 'A debutante, Miss Lambert'. Nice decisive little lasses!)

'Laura's career—It would make so much difference. There are scholarships—'Miss Lambert murmured, rising even as she spoke, for Stella Vaizey was murmuring back with a soothing insulting confidence, 'The girls understand. Their father was not very practical.'

Called on for understanding, her daughters looked at Mrs. Vaizey with a probing uncertainty. She cared for them so little they were awed. Their father had translated her to them from time to time; now Laura was obliged to attempt this for herself and Clare. Recently, she had explained: 'She's wonderful, really, it's only that she's unpredictable. But she's unusual because she's not an Australian, I think. You'd be bound to be different, being born in India.'

Clare left her attention and a finger on the blue-ruled page of her homework book, and raised bright-grey eyes to her sister's face. After an empty perusal of this face, which was intently thinking at a pastel portrait of Princess Elizabeth, Clare's eyes dropped deep into the inky problems of trains travelling at sixty, eighty and ninety-five miles an hour between three distant cities.

'Yes,' Laura repeated, frowning at the princess.

'Mmm.' Clare's agreement had the moody, putting-off note of one resisting an alarm-clock, but a part of her

mind was grateful to hear: *wonderful, unpredictable, born India*.
• From *The Watch Tower*, Elizabeth Harrower, pp. 2–3.

In this extract, which is the opening of the book, dialogue is a means of conveying a great deal of information to the reader in a dramatic way, rather than through explanatory narrative. Dialogue is also the mechanism, as it was in the previous example, to move backwards in time for brief flashbacks, as well as being a means to establish characters quickly and vividly. Dialogue is also the device for hearing the thoughts of several different characters in quick succession within the basic structure of the third-person point of view.

• • •

Auntie Elsie fetched guest towels out of the linen press for our hands. My mother said, *These are nice, Else.* Auntie Elsie said they were made in China and my mother said she would never have guessed they were from the East. Auntie Elsie said she had to confess they'd been cheap. My mother said that nevertheless the embroidery was beautifully done and Auntie Elsie said she thought so too, to tell you the truth. She said she'd got them at a sale at the shop up at the Junction and my mother said *Did you really?* and wasn't that the kettle she heard? Auntie Elsie had a kettle which you heated on top of the stove and which whistled when it boiled. My mother had a Hotpoint electric jug.

Over afternoon tea, my mother and Auntie Elsie discussed how late it was to be having afternoon tea. Then they discussed the china, which was the cups, saucers and plates. The china had not come from China but from England. The point about it, though, was that it had not come from Japan. My Uncle Bert had been in the War, had fought against the Japs in New Guinea, wouldn't have any Jap stuff in the house. My mother considered the Jap stuff inferior anyway and wouldn't buy anything but English herself. She said she thought you could always tell the good stuff. She turned her saucer upside down and studied it sagely, then praised the elegance of Elsie's cups. My mother and Auntie Elsie agreed that you had to be very careful when buying as the Japs were a cunning lot, named the blocks of land where their factories were things like *Derby* and *Staffordshire* and *England,* and then stamped *Made in England* (or whatever it was) on the china, bold as brass, adding *Japan* in smaller letters in a less conspicuous place. They cited various instances of this sort of thing that they'd heard of or read about.

• From *Regards to the Czar*, Margaret Coombs, p. 66.

If this passage was written as direct rather than indirect speech, what would change? Is there something about the use of indirect speech here that gives it an ironic tone?

• • •

The conversation; both standing face to face:
Tania: Twitch of the right thumb.
Helen: Laughter. Her expression gradually declining to that limp seriousness with which one observes a blade of grass.
Tania: Right foot slides a centimetre to the right rear, turning her body slightly away. Looks down. The pub carpet is swept only once a day.
Helen: Silence. Eyes held wide, like a fish rampant.
Tania: Her eyes come up to the level of a breast, linger casually, for they have seen one million two hundred thousand four hundred and ninety-one breasts (well, they *may* have! How could I possibly know?) then arrive at the chin. A scar is all that remains of a once prominent mole. Meant to be off-putting?
Helen: Determination expressed through a slight straightening of the trunk, not to be put off or put down. A part turn away, not much, not enough to mean her eyes are taken off the antagonist's general area. She can see her body, but is not favouring her with eye contact.
Tania: Her feet move, almost together, to a position in front of Helen. She does not want her to escape from greed of eyes—a message?—and need of touch and encirclement. And perhaps control. Or if not control, mutuality. Not a duel: a duet is on the programme.
Helen: Breathes out. She is satisfied Tania has not got control of her whip hand. If she continues to move,

Tania will move to contain her, as she thinks; actually she will follow her. This is natural, for Tania cannot control her unless she has a massive advantage of power over her.

Tania: Her chest seems to be struggling with a need to get words out.

Helen: Her eyes catch the struggling movements, and she waits. What will be necessary to combat this new attack?

End of body conversation; beginning of voice supplement:

> • From *City of Women*, David Ireland, pp. 98–99.

This extract tunes into another kind of language, the language of the body: a conversation where no words are exchanged. What is lost in this way of approaching dialogue, and what is gained?

• • •

'There she is', I say to Bar Holland. We are taking our after-dinner stroll around A Deck.

'Who?'

'*Kaye*. It looks like it's Officers' Night tonight.'

'Chelsea' is dimly lit, but the pink shirt, the white uniforms around it, glow in the light from behind the bar.

'I suppose it's a good way to learn Greek', I say, climbing up the ladder onto Boat Deck behind Bar Holland. There is a railing at the front of Boat Deck, past the funnels, where we always stand. It is as high and far as you can go.

I want to talk about Kaye Garrett with Bar, but something holds me back. 'All that make-up', I want to say, 'do you think she looks *hard*? Do you think she looks older than seventeen? I think swearing is unfeminine. Does she swear in front of men? What is sex-appeal anyway? She's got lots of nice clothes herself, I don't know why she . . .'

It is quieter up here, we are further away from the engine, you can even hear the crisp breaking of the wake, white in the black sea. The wind blows back Bar Holland's beach-white hair from her long, stern chin.

Her eyelashes are white too, so that her stare beyond the ship seems unblinking. I wish that I was like Bar Holland, my mind on higher things.

'Think I'll go down and read', she says.

'Yes', I say, 'I *must* finish my letter'.

Music has started up in the ballroom. The soft thud of the drum, the even ripple of the piano. '*Leesten*', the singer's voice crackles as he adjusts the microphone, '*do you want to know a see-gret?*'

Corridor by corridor we descend the ship.

We went to the ballroom once, on our first night aboard. Kaye was with us then. We sat at a table by the dance-floor and ordered drinks. 'To us', Kaye said. The band, in midnight-blue tuxedos, winked and bowed at us. There was a solo on the electric guitar, the theme song from 'Bonanza'. A middle-aged couple danced a professional tango under the swirling gold hexagons of the dome in the middle of the ceiling.

'Oh my God', Kaye Garrett said, 'This is *dire*.'

But after a while the ballroom filled with people, Second Sitting people. The band took off their coats. The dance floor thronged, lights dimmed, shadows raced around the walls. A white uniform bowed before Kaye. She got up slowly, her face was severe over his shoulder as they circled the floor. Bar Holland and I sipped our drinks, islanded amongst empty tables and chairs. Bar Holland stood up.

'I'm going', she said. 'I'm bored.'

We made a great show of fanning ourselves on the deck, of gasping for fresh air.

> • From 'Sister Ships', Joan London, in
> *Sister Ships*, p. 12.

This extract uses dialogue for several different functions. There's straightforward speech between two characters, as in the first few lines. Then there's dialogue imagined but not spoken, revealing the character to the reader but not to the other character, as when the narrator wants to talk about Kaye Garrett and imagines what she would say. What do we learn about the characters, and their relationship to each other, in the exchange: ' "Think I'll go down and read", she says. "Yes", I say, "I *must* finish my letter".' What's the effect of the italics?

Dialogue is also used to make a moment of the past vivid: the last two paragraphs are not just a flat summary of a past event, but come to life through the dialogue with the immediacy of an event in the present.

• • •

I've come to apologise, I'll say. And I'd like to talk to you. Be your friend.

I'll stand one foot on the path, one foot on the step, encouraged by the white raffia unravelling under her. She'll squint into the light, her hand surprised and shading her eyes.

Or I'll lean on the verandah wall, gazing into the garden as if looking for something forgotten amongst the precise stonework.

I live alone with my father, I'll say. I have for years. So I'm not good at talking to people.

She'll lower her hand, look down to the quarry tiles in squares on the floor. Leaves will drift on the shorn grass.

Rest your legs, she'll say. The chair will scrape, but her hand pushing it will be gentle.

I walk past the house again and again but she's not there. Again and again I walk round the block but it's merely to smell the petrol spills at the garage and watch at the ice-works the rattling slats of a wooden conveyor belt, the white blocks steaming in the light.

But this afternoon, brown with heat, she's there, alone, reading a book, her hair hanging over her face, absorbed. I walk to her gate, falter, walk past. The clouds are heavy, growling, it'll rain soon and jostle people on shining streets into an impromptu familiarity. Afterwards they'll separate, laughing, eyes cast down, remembering they have homes to go to, front doors to bolt, but only afterwards. Because of the clouds, I push the gate open.

She watches as I walk up the path. Lightning jags over the distant traffic. I'd forgotten how far the house was from the road. I'll call hello when I get to that bush with leaves limp as silent tongues. To those drooping poppies.

What are you doing here? she shouts.

Too late I call hello.

She puts down her book.

It's the weirdo, she yells into the house. Lightning slits the sky and is gone, so I'm unsure.

This is private property, she shouts.

I reach for words, like feeling down into a purse, down, down, but everything is zippered up, and when I get the zips to work, the purse is filled with air and the top of my head gapes.

I am close enough to see the cover of her book. The title. True, I read. Confessions. Squeezed out of me by the traitorous clouds.

I wanted to ask you, I shout, and trails of rehearsed words come to me,

because I thought you'd know.

Her head is bent low, her lower eyelids droop to take in the sight of my red face struggling for sense against the bursting sky.

You must know, I shout, and my certainty spirals between her chin and forehead, and fades.

Edward and Russell are framed in the doorway, watching. She looks back at them and her eyelids are tight and she and Edward and Russell are enclosed together and I am alone, open, under the intolerable rain which ricochets around me and shudders across the lawn.

• From *Painted Woman*, Sue Woolfe, p. 70.

The narrator of this extract is a lonely schoolgirl, isolated by the fact that her mother is dead and her father is considered eccentric. The extract uses an unconventional way of punctuating the dialogue. How does that affect the tone? Try reading it aloud and see what sort of tone of voice you find yourself adopting. Although dialogue and narrative run into each other, it's always clear who's speaking — how has the writer ensured this?

One of the underlying themes of *Painted Woman* is the relationship between life and art, and between art and violence. The scene acts out this theme in miniature: the narrator rehearses a reassuring and orderly conversation, but the reality is not only hostile but takes a turn she hasn't foreseen. The artificial conversation she's invented crumbles in the face of the violence and disorder of real life.

•••

The dinner party.

'How do you manage without the language?' asks Leon of Judy as the others order. 'Does Noel speak Italian?'

'He can say "Does anyone here speak English?" but he says that in German and French too.'

'Listen Professor. If I order spaghetti with clams, do I have to take all the clams out of the shells?'

'You lazy son of a bitch! He has energy for some things.'

'I don't know if this might interest you Leon, but this is a photo of my wombat.'

'Goodness! Look at this, Cortesana. And who's this young chap?'

'My son Byron, Noel's son. My friend Wendy...'

'Have you seen Byron's writing desk, Noel? He lived in the middle Mocenigo palace. Browning, of course, died in the Rezzonico, but once owned the Montecuculi.'

'Those were the days, eh champion? You're sure we can't tempt you? No? They do a very good fish soup.'

'And they can be house-trained?'

'Actually, he was named after Byron Bay. That's where he was conceived.'

'I think I've been there, haven't I? Is there an old bath house under the amusement pier?'

'Let me see that photograph. Big teeth like a beaver. You can't house-train herbivores. Hey ah... young lady, would I be right in thinking this creature eats roots and shoots?'

'That sounds more like our champion. Only tonight he's left his gat at home and he's off his tucker.'

'Don't you start in on me. I'll give you what you should have had the other night.'

'How very pleasant this is for me, to be sitting back enjoying such wonderful company. Red wine or white?'

'Shame you can't speak the language, Noel.'

'Only time I miss it is when I'm crossing a bridge near an inter-section and a boatman yells out wanting to know if there's something coming the other way. For the most part, I get the impression it's a language in which you could talk for a long time without saying much.'

'Come on now, you're a guest here fella!'

'So are you.'

'I wouldn't say I was a guest. Would you say I was a guest, Leon?'

'Jolly good, here comes the food. Che bellissimo! Che fantastico!'

'Will you stop staring at that woman? I've never felt so embarrassed.'

'One's first impressions are *so* important, don't you agree Colt?'

'Have you been to the Ducal Palace yet?'

'My bladder wouldn't let me get as far as that on the first day. Go into a bar here to ease your bladder and they top it up before you leave.'

'What most impressed our champion there?'

'The snake trap.'

'Beg pardon?'

'This food is terrible.'

'I think it's a beautiful little animal. Can I have the red wine please?'

• From *Testostero*, David Foster, p. 18.

•••

The setting of this extract is a dinner party in Venice, with Australians, Britons and Italians present. This is an example of sound-track as story; in this scene, dialogue is capable of carrying the whole burden of storytelling, at least for a time. What are the strengths and limitations of this device?

Writers have imaginations that bother them. The more bother the better, but when dealing with the law enforcement authorities on the telephone it is difficult to get down to tin tacks. They think you are making it all up. I, myself, had to execute the leap i thought only the cat of our household was really equipped to do. I fell over, twisting my already weak right ankle. But worse than that, far worse, here was i hunched and slumped on the floor face to face with a dead man in the hallway of my home. I struggled in the end to the telephone and i panted into the handpiece. I thought i was on television, i said i wanted homocide. They started asking questions which required answers that were farthest from my mind. I said i didn't need another homocide as i already had one. In my hallway. Where? Well not far from the front door. You can see it almost *as* you are opening the door. I thought on the phone that that was a real tin tack, the preposition 'as' implied that the body was there *before* i, or any consequent entrant, came in. How long? The question made no sense to me whatsoever. I said, quite frivolously i admit, i bet it's a 172 centimetre one. They all seem to be these days.

• • •

'I'm a writer', i confide to the lady in blue, 'sometimes my etymology, my epistemology, my imagination et cetera run out of hand, i mean get out of control...' I was trying to explain why i had been so frivolous on the telephone to Emergency about the 'as' and the length of time being the length of body. 'I really couldn't tell if he was a 172 centimetres, you see he's all hunched up. He's blocking my passage!' I shouted a little, appealing to her as a woman, even though her being in uniform indicated that she was a junior, the social worker of the three. She stood steadfast, grasping my bag as if it were hers. I turned my attention to the gentlemen. I could see in their eyes that they believed i did it. Already, quite obviously, they were convinced.

'The body was there', i began calmly. 'When i opened the door, in fact, as i was opening the door i saw it.' 'Which time?' the taller man barked. Yes, he barked. And i responded indignantly,'Well, each time, of course'.

Then through the corner of my eye i saw what they were looking at. The number of footprints on the hulk's back had multiplied. I pretended not to be nonplussed. The cigarette burnt between my fore- and ring-fingers. Now i was confused. The policewoman still held my bag.

I speak out, saying i am the one who is dead, he you can see but you are looking through me as if i weren't one of this crowd in the doorway and i know it's the right address, my address. I am she who telephoned and gave you this address. I am the hostess of this investigation and you treat me like a criminal it has taken your nous and resources to discover. Well, uncover me, find me, hear my incessant chatter. It's not only nonsense. I fall down on the body, my companion in suspense, and weep.

119

The policewoman speaks in a voice not hers, a bleak voice. She says, i hear her say, 'Did you love him?'
- From 'Waiting for Colombo', Finola Moorhead, in *Room to Move*, pp. 148–149 and 150–151.

In this extract, a realistic illusion of real speech is not the primary aim of the writer. One effect of the stylised dialogue is to draw attention to the slipperiness of words (in the misunderstanding about 'How long') and their inadequacy to convey almost anything at all. In the context of a non-realistic story, this acknowledgement of the fallibility of words extends not just to the dialogue but to the narrative as well. There is no doubt that what we are reading here is an artificial construct, a story. At the same time, the story is true of the way things are, in a way we can recognise: this story is true to life in a way, although it is not true to traditional fiction.

D IALOGUE that's completely invented, with no reference to real speech, is likely to be over-correct and a bit
dull. The speech of real life is usually energetic, quirky and
surprising. Writers might as well borrow some of that
energy if they can.

6.1   Record a chunk of real conversation somewhere. It can
be between strangers, or people you know. There can
be as many people talking as you like. You can be one
of the speakers if you wish. Recording it on tape makes
it easy.

Then transcribe it as accurately as you can into
writing, putting in all the ums and ers and the parts
where it goes vague and imcomprehensible.

It's very rare for a piece of real speech to have nothing
interesting about it at all, because real human beings have
to work quite hard to be totally without interest. What's
interesting might not be what the speakers thought was
interesting, of course.

The first thing is to isolate what's good about the speech
in the transcript, or at least what's least dull. What's good
might only be one phrase, but that's enough to be going on
with. Ask these questions:

1 Which parts of the transcript, if any, already work on the
written page?
2 What is it that makes those parts interesting?
   • Is it the subject of the conversation? Are interesting
     ideas being expressed, interesting anecdotes being told?
   • Is it the situation? Are they having a conversation in a
     falling lift or while hitting each other over the head?
   • Is it the characters themselves? Do they sound like
     interesting people?

- Is it the language that's interesting? Is it slangy, dialect, vivid, a bit mad?
- Is it unintentionally interesting: so repetitious or rambling that it ends up being funny? Full of tantalising half-finished sentences that make you want to know more?
- Is it funny? What makes it funny, exactly?

Now that you've isolated whatever is interesting about this speech, the next step is to use it as the basis for a piece of fictional dialogue. You'll want to lose all the dull parts and exaggerate whatever that strength is you've found in it. You're likely to find that its strengths are something it would have been hard to invent.

6.2 Re-write the transcript, shaping it to maximise its strengths. Delete the dull parts and reinforce the good parts. If necessary, make it clearer in meaning. This time, write it out as dialogue, using attributions rather than as a simple transcript, and add any gestures, expressions, tones of voice, etc, that are important. If its strength is something about the *way* the people are talking rather than what they're saying, experiment with ways to get this across. Exaggerate everything for the sake of this exercise.

This is now an edited version of reality. The next step is to make the leap into fiction, which may use very little of this real speech. Think about these choices that you might make:
- Would you use realistic or stylized dialogue?
- Would you use direct or indirect speech? Try both, to see the difference it makes.
- Would you add more narration, and reduce the dialogue to a few lines? Or would you keep it almost all dialogue?
- Would you streamline it down to its basics, or would you allow it to blossom into a full-blown scene?
- Would you delete any characters, or add more? Would you combine several characters into one?
- How would you use punctuation?
- How would you use attribution?

6.3 Re-write the dialogue, experimenting with these possibilities. For the sake of the exercise, make as many kinds of changes as you can.

Now the real test: read it aloud. Even better, get someone to read it aloud to you. Make a note of where they stumbled, where the words went together awkwardly, where the sentence was too long or complicated to keep track of, where the words made unintentional rhymes or repeated sounds. Above all, just listen to whether it 'sounds right'. If it doesn't, it isn't.

Building your story

F IRST go through the exercises you've just done and see if there's anything in them that might be useful in your story. It could be a character, a phrase, a setting or just a mood.

By now you've probably already written some dialogue as part of your developing story. For the moment, focus on one scene in your story that contains dialogue.

First, think about what function the dialogue might be serving in your final story. Does it reveal character or make a scene more dramatic or is it where the humour happens?

Next, go through and mark whatever you think is valuable in the dialogue you've already written. It might be a few words or it might be the whole piece.

Assess it in the same way you looked at the raw transcript in the first exercise for this chapter, sifting through for anything promising.

Now think about ways of altering your existing dialogue so that it focuses better on its function and enhances the strengths it already has. Ask these questions:
- What is the dialogue doing in this story?
- Does each voice suit each different character or are they all the same?
- Are the sentences too long or too unvaried in structure?
- Have you used contractions?
- Is it lively, or is it just a bit of filler?
- Is it written with energetic use of language, or is it flat and bland?
- Does it labour along under the weight of too much information being conveyed?

Try:
- Borrowing voices from real life that have distinct mannerisms, to make your characters' voices different.
- Replacing flat or dull language with lively language — try to make it surprising. It's true that real people are often boring, but your story doesn't have to be.
- Writing the dialogue with no sentences longer than six

124

words, no punctuation other than full stops and no words of more than two syllables.

- Interspersing the dialogue with actions or thoughts.
- Omitting some thoughts so that the dialogue leap-frogs rather than flows logically.
- Seeing what happens when you leave out some verbs, leave sentences unfinished and generally abandon grammar.
- Experiment with different punctuation: dots and dashes, exclamation marks, italics, block letters.

You may find that what you had in the first place is best of all but you'll probably find ways to refine it by experimenting in the ways outlined here.

Each time you change it, read it out loud. Listen to the emphasis you're putting on certain words, the pauses you're leaving, the tone of voice in general. Have you found a way of writing it down so that a reader coming freshly to the dialogue would know where to put the emphasis, where to leave a pause, and so on? The test is not whether you can make it sound right when you read it yourself but whether a first-time reader could make it sound right.

If you've tried all these ideas and your scene still hasn't come to life, consider the possibility that this shouldn't be a dialogue scene at all. Perhaps this scene would be better presented in another way.

Try:
- Writing the scene as indirect dialogue.
- Writing the scene with no dialogue at all. You may find that it works better told as straight narrative, with descriptions, thoughts, and actions taking the place of dialogue.
- If this is impossible, or if it doesn't seem to work, that will tell you a great deal about the function of the dialogue in the scene. Why is it so vital? What, exactly, is it doing that can't be done any other way? Once you can clarify the function of the dialogue, you can focus on that function and make sure it's doing it as well as it can.

Now start from the opposite pole. Take a scene in your embryonic story where there's no dialogue: a purely narrative scene. See what happens when you dramatise it by writing it in the form of dialogue.

Imagine this is a play or a film script you're writing rather than a story. Make the scene work purely by what people say and what they do: no explanations, no narrative. In doing this, you may be forced to clarify characters and mention specifics rather than generalities. You may find that you can do without some explanations or background which you thought were necessary. On the other hand, you may find that the heart of the scene is lost when it's reduced to nothing more than dialogue and actions. What, exactly, is lost? A tone of voice from the narrator? Irony? A broad vision that transcends the immediate action? Once you can see what you've lost, you can re-write knowing what's important to the scene.

We began these exercises with a piece of real speech and borrowed its energy for the exercises. If the dialogue in your story is a bit drab or wooden, you may be able to give it an infusion of real-life energy. This experiment may seem like mixing oil and water but try it and see what happens:

Look at the real-life conversation you transcribed for the first exercise. Imagine that two of the characters from your story are having this conversation. Write a short scene in which your characters are using the actual words of your transcribed conversation.

It may be an astonishing new view of your characters to put real speech, from real life, into their mouths. It's likely to point up in a very dramatic way whether their invented speech sounds right. If it doesn't, it will let you hear much more clearly how their voices should sound.

Depending on how advanced your embryonic story is, you may not be quite sure where dialogue will fit in the overall shape of the finished piece. But the only way to discover what a story is, is to keep on writing until the story reveals itself to you. Be as free as you can with these experiments and even try things that you feel sure won't work. Surprising things may happen. With writing, even if you follow many false leads, nothing is wasted in the end.

7. Description

DESCRIPTIONS can be boring set-pieces that you skip in a book. They can feel like padding, or one of the necessary but dull rules of writing fiction. On the other hand, a description can emerge so seamlessly out of a piece of writing that you're not even aware that you've just read one.

Description is never neutral. A description is a series of choices; some details are mentioned, others are not. The describer is doing the choosing, so the description will reveal the describer as much as the described. Depending on the point of view, that describer may be a detached observer, or a character in the story.

Why do you need descriptions?

Description can carry a lot of different loads. At its most basic level, a description can tell the reader necessary information about the thing or person being described. A description can also act as an overture to a piece of fiction, stating some of the themes to follow, and establishing a mood. In this case the thing or person being described might not be particularly significant to the central story, but might set the tone for what follows.

Perhaps most importantly, a description can tell us a great deal about the describer, and the describer's attitude to the thing or person described.

The writing book

What to put in, what to leave out?

The individual items in a description aren't usually interesting in themselves. They're interesting when they add up to a coherent picture. If a description is just a list of details, the end result can be diffuse.

To end up with a description that focuses the reader in the direction you want, you might have to start by putting in every detail you can think of. At a later stage, as the story's themes and moods emerge, you can go back and shape that description, adding some details, taking some out, and changing others, so that the individual details go together to create the effect you want.

Where should a description go?

Description is seldom very dramatic, so if a piece of writing starts with a description it has to be intriguing in some way in its own right, otherwise the reader's interest may fade before the action starts. A description doesn't have to be one unrelieved lump: it can take the form of a gradual build-up of a picture, interspersed with actions or dialogue. The example from Glenda Adams on pp. 130–131 is a description of a suburban backyard, which could be dull but Adams makes it quirky and funny. In this scene, the opening of the book, we meet several main characters and many of the themes of the book are foreshadowed in this description.

Adjectives and adverbs

One of the hard things about writing descriptions, especially of characters, is the difficulty of getting away from clichés. Eyes sparkle and dance, hair is tousled, chins are determined. The other temptation in a description is to fall back on summary words: the room was untidy, the woman was pretty. Both of these problems arise in part from an over-reliance on adverbs and adjectives.

Adverbs and adjectives are often a shorthand: one word can summarise many details which add up to an effect that can be labelled 'pretty', or 'determined'. Being summaries, they're often vague and unspecific. That tends to make them boring. If you work towards reducing adverbs and adjectives, you're forced to look freshly at what you're describing. You're forced to look again and work out just why the eyes appear to sparkle or what makes the chin look determined. In the course of doing that, you're more likely to come across a fresh perception or a new way of summarising it. That's likely to be refreshing, rather than numbing as clichés are.

Naturally, descriptions need some adjectives and adverbs and not all adjectives and adverbs are vague or bland. But the quickest way to restore a dying description to life is to reconsider the adjectives and adverbs.

Image as description

This brings up another way of approaching description: by imagery rather than factual detail. You may come to a dead-end by continuing to try to find details that are going to get something across, where one image might do all the work for you. Look at the example from Peter Carey on pp. 133–134. The image of Joel as 'something over-ripe and gone to seed' draws a more vivid picture than a page of details would be likely to. That image or metaphor then ties together all the other details in the description and gives rise to other images all drawing on the central idea of over-ripe, almost–decaying growth.

Description as attitude

The sub-text in a description is information about the narrator doing the describing, and that narrator's attitude to the thing or person being described. This secondary layer is often what gives a good description its interest. This is true of the Carey example: the choice of image — not repugnant, but threatening to be — directs the reader's response to the character.

Even clearer is the example from Murray Bail on pp. 134–135: we learn what the drover's wife looks like through her husband's eyes, but the interest of the description lies not in the drover's wife herself but in the attitude of her husband and what he reveals about himself. Used like this, a description is an excellent way for the writer to direct the reader's response and introduce irony, without baldly telling the reader what to think: a good description can be worth a thousand explanations.

Examples

THE rooster was crowing, at two in the afternoon, and the cicadas had started up again after their lunchtime quiet.

'It's a case of too much noise,' said Henry Watter, the father of Lark. 'Far too much noise.' He was in the basement working on his project. He seized the hammer and rushed into the backyard. He thrust the rooster into the small wooden crate that rested under the gum tree within the circle of chicken wire that formed its coop and hammered it shut, the sun glinting on the hammer-head and on the lenses of his metal-rimmed glasses. The Bakers' dog next door started barking. The rooster continued crowing. From farther off came the buzz of a lawn-mower.

Lark watched the hammering, then went back to looking through the old seventy-eights and the sheet music stacked near the pianola—Caruso singing '*Vesti la giubba*,' a silly song called 'I Lift Up My Finger and I Say Tweet, Tweet,' and polonaises and rhapsodies played by Ignaz Friedman. She had already saved a hundred pounds, almost enough for a one-way passage to somewhere, Singapore or Ceylon perhaps, and she had arranged for an interview with Qantas to be an air hostess, after her exams. That was one way to get away.

Lark's father rushed into the house, then returned to the backyard with several army blankets and a tattered French flag, which he draped over the crate, layer on layer, creating night for the confused bird.

'Sits there like a stunned mullet,' said Henry Watter.

'Do you think that's wise, Henry?' asked Lark's mother from under her pink cloth sunhat. Her hands, in white gloves, were pegging clothes on the line with such alacrity that she could have been playing a scherzo on the pianola. The gloves protected her hands from the sun. The sunhat, in addition to performing its intended function, protected her head from the kookaburras and magpies, which liked to swoop down to take strands of hair for their nests.

'Like bombers,' said Henry Watter. 'It's a case of World War Two in our own backyard. This country's a joke. One big joke.'
  • From *Dancing on Coral*, Glenda Adams, p. 1.

There's an intensity about this description of a suburban backyard that comes from the fact that nothing is vague or generalised. Everything is drawn with absolute precision, even the names of the songs on the records and the kind of blankets. There is a hectic effect created by all this intense detail which almost makes the page noisy, as the scene is.

The only unspecific thing mentioned here is Henry's 'project'. The extreme vagueness of this in the midst of such tight-packed details is a clue that this 'project' will become a significant mystery later in the book.

Notice how the impression of Father as the centre of furious activity is increased by the very dynamic verbs associated with him (he seized, rushed, thrust, hammered, etc). By contrast, the verbs associated with Lark and her mother are relatively static: watched, looked through, etc.

Notice how different kinds of sounds are being heard or referred to (in the case of the old seventy-eights and the imagined scherzo on the pianola). No wonder Lark is wondering how to get away.

• • •

Father Greely had been a spiritual investigator, the very private eye of ecclesiastical courts, for years. Padding across the tarmacs of airport terminals, through the spurious security of plastic and nylon carpeting in Gauguin colours that went with the terminal bars, he was a sinister figure in his black, much given to gaberdine overcoats and overstuffed briefcases. The nose, the formidable jaw, the baggy eyes and the hard mouth gave nothing away—he was a dangerous poker player —while his habit of reading a paper and watching over the top of it the farewelling unmarried couples gave his whole person an ambience of espionage. He carried his job like a disease.

Now, having left the others by the Burns Philp Stores, under the awnings with their cameras clicking like crickets, he came up the main street along the waterfront, his bulging grip clinging to official letters, two changes of underwear, three pairs of socks, an admonitory letter from the bishop and a secret communication from the provincial of the area. His strangeness attracted natives like flies. He was buzzed about by children and tried to smile, although the heat and the nuisance of it all were making him inwardly whimper.

'Off now! Off now!' he kept saying as unbrusquely as he could manage, patting the thick air about him with his free hand. Not once did he think consciously of what he would have to say, to do, although those very things were all round him like climate. Or love. He did not know much about love, imagining from the cruciform tower where his bleak eyes watched the world that folk disported themselves as challenge to challenge. The bliss flaked off within months and there they were, the contestants, one battered, one victor, and the ropes sagging all round the ring. But when the beaten and the conqueror looked out over the crowd, faces were turned away, their souls or the features of them in shadow, and they too were all in pairs, wounding, striking, accepting.

He wiped his face on his fourth handkerchief— Deladier had warned him things dried so fast in the heat there was no need to bring too much—and he swung right between the big store that sold plastic gimcrackery to the natives and the offices of Air-Torres, and paced steadily up the hill towards the mission buildings and Father Lake's doom.

- From *A Boatload of Home Folk*, Thea Astley, p. 56.

This begins as a straight physical description, but it avoids the feeling of a set–piece because of the way it modulates subtly into action. In fact, the whole description is full of action: Father Greely isn't a static figure having his portrait painted, but a man being observed as he moves; and the way he moves reveals him to us. Every detail is crisp: nothing is described in a vague or general way. We know just what kind of overcoat he wears and just what his briefcase looks like. When the description verges on a summary—'formidable jaw', 'hard mouth'—it's rescued immediately by a vivid image that brings it into sharp focus again: 'he was a dangerous poker player'.

There's a gusto and flamboyance about the imagery: it's a series of small shocks of vividness, throwing up one picture after another, each as startling and convincing as the last.

• • •

Harry Joy was to die three times, but it was his first death which was to have the greatest effect on him, and it is this first death which we shall now witness.

There is Harry Joy lying in the middle of that green suburban lawn, beneath that tattered banana tree, partly obscured by the frangipani, which even now drops a single sweet flower beside his slightly grey face.

As usual Harry is wearing a grubby white suit, and as he lies there, quite dead, his blue braces are visible to all the world and anyone can see that he has sewn on one of those buttons himself rather than ask his wife. He has a thin face and at the moment it looks peaceful enough. It is only the acute angles struck by his long gangling limbs which announce the suddenness of his departure. His cheeks are slightly sunken, and his large moustache (a moustache far too big for such a thin face) covers his mouth and leaves its expression as enigmatic as ever. His straight grey hair, the colour of an empty ashtray, hangs over one eye. And, although no one seems to have noticed it, a cigarette still burns between two yellowed fingers, like some practical joke known to raise the dead.

• • •

Joel bared his teeth in return and checked his cufflinks, a salesman's habit he would have done well to be rid of. He did other American things (for he was an American), like insisting on iced water at table and then drinking spirits throughout the meal, which was noticed by everybody and not always approved of. The town had an ambivalent attitude towards Americans, envying their power and wishing to reject it and embrace it all at once. In business you could never be sure whether it was an asset or a liability to be an American.

Joel was only twenty-six but there was about him the sense of something over-ripe and gone to seed. He was not tall, and not exactly fat. But one noticed, immediately, those large red lips, which hovered on that balancing point where sensuality becomes greed. His fleshy face was a trifle too smooth and the skin glistened like a suspect apple which had been waxed to give it extra sales appeal.

● From *Bliss*, Peter Carey, pp. 1 and 11.

Whereas Thea Astley bombards us with a variety of images, Peter Carey uses imagery all of the same kind to create a cumulative effect. The description of Harry Joy lying on the lawn begins with images of colours and things growing: Harry Joy is part of a garden tableau, linked to nature. Then the description modulates to a less harmonious set of images: hollow cheeks and awkward angles are not in harmony with the natural world around him. That brings us to the third part of the description, with its ashtray image. This movement in the imagery foreshadows a theme of the book: Harry Joy is an advertising man who promotes dubious products, but by the end of the book he's living in the bush, planting trees.

The description of Joel is carefully shaped around a central, consistent image, also of plants. It's appropriate that these two men are linked by imagery, because Joel is having an affair with Harry Joy's wife. Harry Joy's plant images are healthy, however, whereas Joel's plant images are rotten.

● ● ●

There has perhaps been a mistake—but of no great importance—made in the denomination of this picture. The woman depicted is not 'The Drover's Wife'. She is my wife. We have not seen each other now . . . it must be getting on thirty years. This portrait was painted shortly after she left—and had joined him. Notice she has very conveniently hidden her wedding hand. It is a canvas 20 × 24 inches, signed l/r 'Russell Drysdale'.

I say 'shortly after' because she has our small suit-case—Drysdale has made it look like a shopping bag—and she is wearing the sandshoes she normally wore to the beach. Besides, it is dated 1945.

It is Hazel alright.

How much can you tell by a face? That a woman has left a husband and two children? Here, I think the artist has fallen down (though how was he to know?). He has

Hazel with a resigned helpless expression — as if it was all my fault. Or, as if she had been a country woman all her ruddy life.

Otherwise the likeness is fair enough.

Hazel was large-boned. Our last argument I remember concerned her weight. She weighed — I have the figures — 12st. 4 ozs. And she wasn't exactly tall. I see that she put it back on almost immediately. It doesn't take long. See her legs.

She had a small, pretty face, I'll give her that. I was always surprised by her eyes. How solemn they were. The painting shows that. Overall, a gentle face, one that other women liked. How long it must have lasted up in the drought conditions is anybody's guess.

> • From 'The Drover's Wife', Murray Bail, in
> *The Drover's Wife*, p. 58.

In the extract from *Bliss*, the imagery affected our attitude towards the characters. In 'The Drover's Wife', the grudging tone of voice, and the unflattering details the narrator chooses to mention, make the narrator's attitude perfectly clear. But is the reader's attitude necessarily the same as the narrator's? Notice how much we learn about this narrator's character and history, as well as that of his wife, just from the description of the painting.

• • •

The year was starched by heat, but they swam on a road ground smoother than any spice. Ahead the town was layered carelessly from the flat with its rows of Chinese shops in ambuscade, to a fading cross on the hospital up the slope. A swat of clay roofing here and there, a bent cathedral cross — hit by cyclones, or fighting — and all this against the diminishing scale of the Tagua Mountains, with fine edges of smoke rising from scattered fires where the natives were burning off. Ranse looked about, at a familiar but alien landscape. *If it's not Asia, where are these people from and where are they going?* Their platform had floated across Oceania, absorbing all the physical cultures it could find: the birdlife and outrageous plants, miniature kangaroos and tropical frictions wherever they existed. But resting now off the northern

hints of Australia's enormous bodyweight and leather
gums. And only the toughest eucalypts cling to granite
cracks here, he thought, on this side of the Shark Nest
Sea that separates them from us. Everything about it
was slightly different, and empty. The air itself, not
even yesterday's air from Asia coming down to stifle
them; but so dry it smelled of nothing. Except the vague
emotional vacuum he found himself in. His nostrils gave
up, and eyelids lowered to a blur. Did it really belong to
his earlier days, or was the discomfort born simply from
the bandaged rhythms of the jeep? The epidural landscape would always surface, from time to time. And
now da Cunha was driving somewhere to test him
against the heat fatigue of getting there: simply that, or
what?

• From *The Children Must Dance*, Tony Maniaty, p. 8.

This description moves gradually from the external to the
internal. It begins with a description of a landscape. Then
the character observes and describes the landscape, and
finally reveals how the mood of the landscape reflects his
own mood. There's a sense of being gradually drawn into
the character's state of mind, a slow movement from the
world of things to the world of thoughts: description of the
physical world is the means of moving between those two
worlds.

Exercises

N o description includes every single detail. Description is a matter of making choices: the choice of what to put in, and what to leave out, is the writer's. Everyone's living-room is pretty much the same, but ask twenty people to describe their living-rooms and you'll get twenty different descriptions.

7.1   Describe your living-room in a few paragraphs.

You've chosen to mention a particular set of details: another person might have chosen a different set. Think about why you chose to mention the things you did and why you left out the things you did. Does that say something about you as well as something about your living-room?

This is an undirected description: a description in limbo. Can it be made to reveal something further? First, can it reveal something more about itself?

7.2   Re-write this description, using basically the same information, but change whatever you need to so that the reader can guess at what has just been happening in the room. Use all the senses. You'll have to start inventing here, adding to the real information with pieces that you make up and leaving out anything that works against what you're trying to convey.

Instead of having to tell the reader what's been going on, you can let the description do so in an oblique way which may be more interesting.

There's a second level that the description can reveal: something about the narrator doing the describing.

7.3 Re-write the description, showing not only what has just been happening in the room, but how the narrator feels about what has just been happening in the room. Here you might have to cut the umbilical cord with reality and start inventing. You might have to change what has been happening. You will probably choose different kinds of words, perhaps more emotive ones. You may vary the sentence structure by using, for example, exclamations, questions, very short sentences, and so on. You may find an image to focus the feeling. Remember, make sure you're still describing the room, not describing feelings.

What about people? In Chapter 3, you wrote several descriptions of people. Choose one of them, and try this:

7.4 Re-write the description without using any adjectives or adverbs.

This will force you to be very specific, and to 'show' rather than 'tell'. If the character looks hungry, or tense, what is it that makes him look that way? Without adjectives and adverbs, you're driven back to verbs as a means of expression and you might find yourself describing the character in terms of actions: body language, gestures, posture, activities. Doing without adjectives and adverbs forces you towards imagery and into the discoveries that you can make when you move away from the literal into the metaphoric. For example, if you find yourself writing 'his hair was the colour of dirt', rather than 'his hair was brown', this is illuminating. Why have you chosen to compare his hair with dirt, of all the things you could have chosen? Does that indicate how you feel about this character, which you mightn't have been aware of before?

As you write, you might find yourself being forced by the restrictions of the exercise to alter your character by inventing new details, things can be described without adjectives and adverbs. You may find yourself writing about another character altogether. Follow where the exercise leads—the new character might be more interesting than the original one.

Now that you have an idea what can be done without adverbs and adjectives, you can choose to put a few back in. They'll be the ones that you really need and they'll also probably be much more vivid than the ones in your first draft, because of the new insights you'll have had by doing without them.

7.5 Re-write the description again, using whatever adverbs and adjectives you wish. You may find that this time you're writing about a third character, a composite of both the earlier ones.

Description can sometimes be a trigger for a story: there's an impulse to write a description, and later on you see where the description will take its place in a story. Try doing that with the two descriptions you have here:

7.6 However unlikely it seems, write a scene in which the character you've just been describing is in the living-room you described earlier. Put the two elements together and see what happens. The more bizarre the combination is, the more likely it is to be interesting. Now, of course, the description will start to become action, as the person and the place start to interact in some way.

Building your story

G o through the exercises you've just done and pick out anything that attracts your attention. Don't worry if you can't see how it will fit into your story, but make a note of it.

Your embryonic story might not look like a story yet, but by now it's a substantial pile of writing. Look through all the pieces until you find something you feel drawn to describe. It might be a person, a place, or an object: it might be a meal or an animal or the weather. It might be obviously important to your story or it might seem marginal. Trust your instinct, and choose something you feel drawn to describing.

Describe whatever you've chosen in some detail. You may find the description sliding into action: make a note of where the action might go, but stick to description for the moment. If the description is of a person, you may find it sliding into judgements or summaries of the character's personality: for the moment, resist this and stick to description of physical attributes. You may find you come to a dead-end very quickly: if so, choose something else to describe. For the moment, don't worry about the focus or significance of the description: think of it as a kind of meditation or survey. In focusing on one element like this, you may see new possibilities for your story: new ideas or associations may emerge.

You may find that your finished story has no descriptions in it at all but, in writing the descriptions, you will have learnt things that you needed to know in order to finish the story.

Ask these questions about the description:

- Does it reveal something beyond itself? Does it reveal how the narrator feels about the thing being described? Does it link up in any way with other parts of the story? Is there a symbolic dimension to the description? Does it reveal something about a character's personality or history? Does it convey a mood?

- What would change if the description used no adjectives or adverbs?
- What would change if some were added?
- What would change if all the verbs were made more dramatic?
- Is this description compelling in itself, or is it flat?
- Does the reader need to know these details to understand the story?
- Would this description be a good way to start the story?

8 Design

P LOTS are important. But they're not what makes you read a book. If plot was all there was to it, it would be enthralling to have someone tell you the plot of a book you haven't read. And having someone tell you the plot of a book you haven't read is hardly ever enthralling. Think of the way some people have the knack of telling a joke well, while someone else can tell the same joke and it falls flat. The difference isn't the joke itself but how it's told. What transforms a plot into a piece of powerful writing is design: not the events themselves but how the events unfold.

Plot

Getting a string of things happening is the basic raw material of a piece of writing. Put them together and you've got a plot.

What makes a good plot? Any kind of plot can be made to work. Some plots present the reader with a series of surprises: others are entirely predictable. Some plots encompass large dramatic actions, others take place within one room. Some stories are dominated by their plots: others have only the sketchiest of plots.

Some writers start with a plot and then flesh it out with characters, places, vivid language, and so on. However, many writers reverse the process and start with their characters, their places, and their language. Then, in later drafts those elements will gradually suggest a plot, which will emerge organically out of the material they have. Both ways can work.

If you start off with a plot, the danger is that it can become a tyrant: in order to stick to the plot, the writer might be forced to distort the characters or ignore interesting ideas that emerge during the writing. If you start off without a plot, the danger is that it might be difficult to come up with one later.

My own feeling is that the second danger is less damaging to the quality of the writing. If thinking of a plot is a real problem, you can always ransack Greek myths or Hollywood movies or stories your grandmother told you until you come up with a plot you can borrow.

However, some of the greatest stories do not have plots. Virtually nothing at all happens, yet there's a powerful sense of character or place or mood or ideas. In such a story, a heavy plot would overwhelm the material.

Plot is one of the most artificial qualities of the artificial construct called fiction. Life doesn't have plot: life just has a flow of events. The only kind of plot that life can offer is a retrospective one. There's nothing wrong with artificial constructs such as plots. But a writer can choose to do without them. A writer can choose to imitate the plotlessness of life and allow the material to be organised in some other way.

Both approaches — to use a strong plot-line, or pare plot down to a minimum — can work, and both can have their dangers. The great danger of the conventional plot is that it becomes so contrived and unlifelike that it becomes dead: a pale, shallow imitation of the richness of real life. The great danger of the plotless narrative is that there isn't enough forward movement for the reader to stay interested.

So, if you choose to stick with a plot of the traditional kind, you have to keep it surprising — which is the quality life has — while avoiding the far-fetched. If you choose to go with minimal plot, you need to provide the reader with some alternative source of interest.

Suspension of disbelief

We touched on this in Chapter 3, in connection with character. Any character can be 'convincing', but the writer has to make them so. Any plot can be 'believable', too, but it has to be made believable. What makes a plot believable is a mixture of things — characters that are alive, language that's vital and suits the characters, and all the other details that make writing live.

Traditional kinds of narrative depend heavily on a suspension of disbelief, because the traditional well-made plot is an artificial thing that the reader is being asked to accept as a slice of real life. Also, those traditional kinds of plots tend to rely on coincidence, neat dove-tailing of events, happy accidents, and so on, and life doesn't have too many of those. Readers are very willing to suspend their disbelief of all these unlikely events because the pay-off is the satisfaction of seeing the story played out, like a game with rules.

However, not all kinds of fiction ask readers to suspend disbelief. Some kinds of fiction constantly draw attention to the fact that it's a story being told rather than a piece of life being lived. Some do this in order to achieve a higher degree of authenticity, a greater authority for the tale. They might be attempting a genuine 'slice of life', an ultimate truthfulness about the way life really moves. Other stories draw attention to themselves as a kind of game: the reader expects the patterns of traditional fiction and those expectations are constantly being subverted.

The highly artificial forms of traditional fiction can feel very 'convincing'. Once the reader has gone into suspension-of-disbelief mode, everything flows very smoothly: nothing interrupts the game, the illusion that this is 'real'.

Paradoxically, the more assertive, less invisible forms of non-traditional fiction often don't feel so 'convincing'. They're not attempting to be smooth and unchallenging: they're attempting to unsettle the reader. They're more like the experience of living than the usual experience of reading.

Lifelike plots

Plots taken straight from life sometimes fall between two stools. They're hardly ever as satisfying as traditional plots because they haven't been shaped towards a final end: they've just happened. They may be weakened by being predictable or by fading away into an anti-climax.

Another paradox is that plots taken directly from real life are often hard to believe: they're 'unconvincing'. Extraordinary, 'unbelievable' things happen in real life but they have to be made believable before they can transfer to the page. It's never enough to say 'but this really happened' to justify a plot, just as it's never enough to say 'but I really know someone like that' to justify a character. The reader has to be saturated with the experience of these events, or that character, before a writer can expect the reader to be convinced.

The plots of conventional fiction usually have an identifiable beginning, middle and end, in that order. Nontraditional fiction may or may not have a beginning, middle and end, and even if it does, they may not happen in that order. Traditionally, a plot can be sometimes described in the form of a graph with various landmarks: initiating incident, complication, rising action, climax, falling action, denouement. But the variety of plots makes the graph too abstract to be very useful. And in non-traditional narratives such a graph becomes irrelevant.

Ways to think about design

1 Event
A story consists of a series of events. The most straightforward way to arrange them is chronologically: first this happened, then this, then this. But that's not the only way and it may not be the best way for your particular story. Here are a few other possible ways of arranging the events.

- End-at-beginning: the first scene is the climax of the story, then the story goes back to some point in the past and moves forward until it catches up with the climax again. The reader learns right in the beginning what happens and spends the story finding out why.
- Telling-the-story-backwards: the story starts with the most recent events, then works progressively backwards, usually in defined sections, to the most distant events. There are really two movements going on: within each section the action moves forward, but the overall movement of the piece is backward.
- Flashbacks: the present action of the story can be inter-

spersed with past events so that the two illuminate each other.

- Subplot: weaving in and out of the main action, a secondary action.
- Parallel stories of equal importance: taking a subplot one step further, into the 'meanwhile back at the ranch' structure. For this to work, both stories need to be equally strong, or the reader starts skipping the weaker one.
- Story-within-a-story: within the main framework of the story, another self-contained story can be told — for example, by one of the characters or in the form of letters or a journal or another device.
- Horizontal or vertical: the story can be a horizontal one, progressing forward along a time-line, or it can be a vertical one — burrowing down into the details of one event over a short space of time.
- Another-turn-of the-screw: at the point where you think the story ends, there may be another possible twist in the plot, another surprise.

2 Secrets
You can ask the question: who knows most about this story?
- Sometimes it's the narrator and sometimes the narrator knows things that he or she is not telling the reader. An example would be the narrator of the Beverley Farmer story on pp. 152–153.
- Sometimes the narrator lets the reader in on the secret but keeps it concealed from other characters in the story: an example would be the narrator of the Robert Drewe story, the ex-convict with the binoculars, on pp. 64–65.
- Sometimes the reader is the one who knows most, as in the example from Murray Bail of the man looking at the painting, 'The Drover's Wife', on pp. 134–135.
- Sometimes a character is the one with the secret, for example, the dark man reading the book in the Tim Winton story on pp. 41–42.

A secret is a great thing for a story. In re-designing a rather flat story, it's likely to become a lot more interesting if you can make sure that not everything is known by everybody. Limit the knowledge in some way: conceal something from someone.

3 Focus

A third part of design is the focus of the piece: some central organising concept that draws the different parts together. Here are some kinds of focus.

- Character: everything in the story illuminates a character or set of characters.
- The punch-line: everything in the story is setting the scene for that ending. Jokes generally have this kind of focus.
- A mood: everything in the story builds up a mood or feeling.
- An abstract idea or theme: the story might take an idea like 'betrayal' or 'conflict between generations' and focus everything towards bringing that abstraction to life.

The focus of a piece is not always the one you intended. You might have thought you were writing a fairly simple story of the punch-line variety, but if you look at it again you might find the real focus of the piece is a character or a mood.

Once you've located or decided on your focus, you can use various devices to emphasise it.

- Repetition: a character might do the same thing over and over, or the narrator might re-tell the same events in different ways or might repeat certain key words many times.
- Unified imagery: every figure of speech, every bit of colourful language, can all be of the same kind. For example, the nature imagery in the Peter Carey extracts on pp. 133–134.
- Symbolism: something in this story might be used as a way of summing up and standing for an idea. For example, polio, and the Mask of Paralysis, becomes a symbol for the battle between the forces of darkness and the forces of light in the extract from Christopher Koch's novel on pp. 153–155.
- Intrusive narrator: the narrator can step out of the flow of events to comment on them in a way that focuses the piece. The narrator can point out the significance of the events described or draw attention to the story-telling process. For example, the extract from Carmel Bird's story on p. 8–9.

- Showing rather than telling: dramatising an idea by letting the reader see it played out, rather than summarised. For example, the 'flashback' within the Joan London extract, pp. 113–114.

A piece of finished fiction often has more than one focus and it's not always easy to say precisely what the focus is: different readers will see the focus of the piece differently. This is part of the richness of good writing but in the early stages it's a helpful exercise to simplify the idea of focus in order to see it clearly.

'**M**RS Porteous, you're done in, aren't you?' I can only nod.

'Look, I'm sorry. I'm really sorry. Standing gas-bagging! I'll get those odds and ends up and then I'll really push off.'

As soon as he goes I sit down hard in the straight-backed chair by the window. It goes without saying that never, never in my life, have I chosen the right clothes for a journey. I am hot in all my silly wool. As I take off my jacket Jack Cust comes back, almost running this time, and looking at me anxiously, as if I may be going to beat him.

'Where do you want them, Mrs Porteous?'

'Just there, thank you, Mr Cust.'

His anxiety changes to indignation. 'But the front bedroom's all fixed up for you.'

'Then please, put everything in there.'

He does. He does that. And at last he goes.

It is wonderful to be able to stop smiling. I feel that ever since setting foot in Australia I have been smiling, and saying, 'Thank you' and 'So kind'. I have one rather contemptible characteristic. In fact, I have many. But never mind the others now. The one I am talking about is my tendency to be a bit of a toady. Whenever I am in an insecure position, that is what happens. I massage the smile from my face by pressing the flesh with my fingertips, over and over again, as I used to do when I had that facelift, all those years ago. I long more than ever for that hot bath, but am too tired to move. I am troubled, too, by guilt, because I was irritable with Jack Cust, who was so kind. I shut my eyes, and when, after a few minutes, I open them again, I find myself looking through the glass on to a miniature landscape of mountains and valleys with a tiny castle, weird and ruined, set on one slope.

That is what I was looking for. But it is not richly green, as it used to be in the queer drenched golden light after the January rains, when these distortions in the cheap thick glass gave me my first intimation of a country as beautiful as those in my childhood books. I would kneel on a chair by this window, and after finding the required angle of vision, such as I found just now by accident, I would keep very still, afraid to move lest I lose it. I was deeply engrossed by those miniature landscapes, green, wet, romantic, with silver serpentine rivulets, and flashing lakes, and castles moulded out of any old stick or stone. I believe they enchanted me. Kneeling on that chair, I was scarcely present at all. My other landscape had absorbed me. And later, when I was mad about poetry, and I read *The Idylls of the King* and *The Lady of Shallot*, and so on and so forth, I already had my Camelot. I no longer looked through the glass. I no longer needed to.

• • •

Often, I used to walk by the river, the real river half a mile from the house. It was broad, brown, and strong, and as I walked beside it I hardly saw it, and never used it as a location for my dreams. Sometimes it overran its banks, and when the flood water receded, mud would be left in all the broad hollows and narrow clefts of the river flats. As soon as this mud became firm, short soft thick tender grass would appear on its surface, making on the green paddocks streaks and ovals of a richer green. One moonlit night, coming home across the paddocks from Olive Partridge's house, I threw down my music case, dropped to the ground, and let myself roll into one of these clefts. I unbuttoned my blouse, unlaced my bodice, and rolled over and over in the sweet grass.

• • •

I wish I had recalled the incident earlier. I should have liked to have recounted it at number six. It would have had to be told at a time when Fred was not there. Fred had that horror of what he called 'fuggy female talk', and although he made a great comedy of it, we all knew that those exaggerated sour mouths, and all that hissing and head-ducking, covered a real detestation, and so we were careful to spare him. No, I should never have recounted the incident in his presence. It would have been told when he was out, or downstairs, and we three were gossiping in Liza's quarters, perhaps, before her new electric fire. And after I had finished, I know what Hilda and Liza would have said. I can hear Liza's voice, with its touch of dogmatism.

'Of course, Nora, you were looking for a lover.'

And Hilda. 'But of course! As girls did in those days, without even knowing it.'

And I would probably have said, yes, of course, because in these times, when sexuality is so very fashionable, it is easy to believe that it underlies all our actions. But really, though I am quite aware of the sexual nature of the incident, I don't believe I was looking for a lover. Or not only for a lover. I believe I was also trying to match that region of my mind, Camelot.

• • •

I had a pinkish skin that always looked damp and often was. In the swampy summers I sweated dread-fully. I changed my dress-shields three or four times a day and washed them secretly. Most of my friends were dry-skinned girls with sun-tanned hands and electrical energy. I remember how Olive Partridge would break suddenly into a run, then as suddenly stop and clack her boots together sideways. But though Olive did things like that when she and I were alone, she was dignified in groups and would not play games. She was never present at those tennis afternoons (called 'the tennis'), when the girls staggered from the court and flopped panting on to the grass, and the boys flopped down beside them and splashed their faces with water from the canvas bags. Ashamed of my sweat, I sat alone in the tennis shed. The girls laughed and shrieked, and I could hear the swishing of cloth as they kicked their legs in their skirts and petticoats. My laughter at the antics of the girls was strained, but in a longing for solidarity I eagerly unhooked the water bag and passed it to the boys. My first touch of toadiness?

• From *Tirra Lirra by the River*, Jessica Anderson, pp. 7–9, 9–10, 10–11, and 11–12.

In these extracts near the beginning of the book, three levels of time are being established: the present (the narra-tor as an old woman arriving back home), recent past (the

narrator's life in England), and the distant past (her childhood). Having set up these three time-zones, Anderson can
then slip around between them for the rest of the book. It's
a kind of flashback structure but a very seamless one. The
book is about an elderly woman who returns to her childhood home, so this musing backwards and forwards along
the line of time is most appropriate.

Have a look at the points where one time-level is joined
onto another. What are the different ways Anderson has
smoothed the transition from one to the other? The opening
of this extract takes place in the present, in which an old
woman arrives after a long trip and a neighbour helps her
into the house. The action of looking out the window is the
mechanism by which thoughts of the past can be introduced
and, in the paragraph that follows, the tense shifts to the
past tense.

Having introduced the general idea of childhood, it's an
easy step to recalling a particular incident from that time, as
happens in the next paragraph: 'Often, I used to walk by
the river . . .'

This incident in turn acts as a device for introducing
another level of time, the recent past: 'I wish I had recalled
the incident earlier.' At the end of this scene in the recent
past, the narrator circles back, via a reference to Camelot, to
the time of childhood and the tennis parties. At the end of
this scene, there is a reference to toadying, which brings us
back to the present, where the narrator feels she's toadied
to Jack Cust.

•••

Her front door locks, but not her back door. Like the
doors on many houses in her suburb, they are panelled
and stained old pine ones, doors solid enough for a
fortress: but the back one opens with a push straight
into her wooden kitchen. Moonlight coats in icy shapes
and shadows the floor and walls which I know to be
golden pine, knotted and scuffed, having seen them in
sunlight and cloudlight as often as I have needed to;
having seen them lamplit too, cut into small gold pictures by the wooden frames of the window, thirty small
panes, while I stood unseen on the back verandah. (The
lampshades are lacy baskets and sway in draughts,
rocking the room as if it were a ship's cabin and the light

off waves at sunset or sunrise washed lacily inside it. Trails like smoke wavering their shadows over the ceiling are not smoke, but cobwebs blowing loose.) These autumn nights she has a log fire burning, and another in her front room just beyond. With the lights all off, the embers shine like glass. They fill the house all night with a warm breath of fire.

An old clock over the kitchen fire chimes the hours. One. Two.

Off the passage from her front room is a wooden staircase. Her two small daughters sleep upstairs, soundly all night. Beyond the staircase a thick door is left half-open: this is her room. In its white walls the three thin windows are slits of green light by day, their curtains of red velvet drawn apart like lips. There is a fireplace, never used; hardly any furniture. A worn rug, one cane armchair, a desk with a lamp stooped over books and papers (children's essays and poems drawn over in coloured pencil, marked in red ink); old books on dark shelves; a bed with a puffed red quilt where she sleeps. Alone, her hair lying in black ripples on the pillow.

• From 'A Woman with Black Hair', Beverley Farmer, in
Home Time, p. 53.

Part of the design of this short story relies on its central secret, which the reader gradually learns. The secret is that the narrator is a rapist who creeps into the house one night and assaults the woman he's been watching. This extract is the first paragraph, which is full of secrets: details that are strange until we know why the narrator has noticed them. There's a peculiar emphasis on whether doors are open or closed: the narrator says, oddly, that he's seen things 'as often as I needed to', and so on. There's a foreshadowing of images that recur later in the story in a more dramatic context: images of cutting, of breathing, of sleeping, of the physical textures of things as if they are being experienced in darkness.

• • •

I was playing with my Hornby clockwork train when the intruder arrived. A toy for which I had a special affection, it ran perfectly, and never broke down: British and reliable.

I had been ill yesterday and today: nothing serious, just a sore throat and a temperature which had kept me home from school. I felt weak and somewhat dreamy and there were dull pains in my back and legs — all the symptoms of 'flu, which was what my mother had decided I'd caught. No one was concerned: least of all me.

There was a fire in the dining-room of my grand-father's house, and I had come out here in my dressing-gown to set up my train on the hearth-rug. I had developed a curious restlessness which I couldn't account for. I was unable to read or to fix my attention on anything for long without a feeling of pointless irritability, mixed with drowsiness. My head ached and there was a stiffness in my neck now, as well as in my back. This ominous symptom, which would have been of great interest to my mother, I supposed to be another feature of the 'flu, and I took no notice of it. But my restlessness increased: I wanted something: some re-assurance perhaps.

About what? I couldn't really tell. The little red loco-motive with its coal truck and two carriages whirred round and round on its silver tracks, recalling happy evenings with my father, before he was killed near Lae. I was safe with my reliable Hornby: and yet I was somehow not reassured. It ran busily through the wooden tunnel my lost father had made for it along ago, and then it began to slow down.

I wanted to reach for the key on the carpet to wind it up again, but I found I was suddenly too heavy and weak to bother doing so. Legs curled under me, I watched the train stupidly as it began another circuit. It laboured down the line towards me, slower and slower, the tension in its clockwork spring almost exhausted. Would it get to me? This somehow seemed very import-ant, and I told myself I would pick it up when it reached me.

It came almost to a stop, but then gave a lurch which brought it forward a few more inches. I badly wanted it to reach me: then things would be all right. But I couldn't move. It stopped just out of reach, and stood there with a distinctness which was no longer friendly.

It was surrounded by an evil emptiness: a speckled vacuum: and I was seized with terror. The world had become reduced to the static red train, the fireplace with its arch of green ceramic tiles containing leaping flames, and the heath-rug's pattern of brown autumn leaves. This pattern, which I had always been fond of, now became entirely unpleasant, and of no help. I wanted to call for my mother, but there was nothing to call out for. I made a great effort and leaned forward to reach for the locomotive.

Pain struck me in the back like a great silver club. I knew immediately that this was no ordinary pain: it had a mighty authority which said that my whole life had been changed: that I had been chosen. I tried to get up, pressing the palm of my right hand flat on the floor.

And now I did cry out—an amazed howl, as the silver club fell again with unbelievable violence, with a force which was obviously intended to punish me for daring to move. Terror established itself absolutely: the speckles in the air increased: the pain entered my bones, so that I understood where each one was. Things were turning off inside me one by one, like lightbulbs. A nasty limpness had arrived, and would stay. I heard my mother's feet running in the hall outside: I fell sideways on the hearth-rug, and entered darkness.

In the hospital, where I was delirious, there were banging noises. When I slept, these noises continued, together with echoing clangs and yells of pain from high corridors of torment outside. My face burned, and the aching in my bones from the blows of the club was still there: I woke into semi-darkness with blue lights and called for my mother, whose face appeared in the uncertainty above me: I begged her to save me from what was happening in the corridors. Then I slept again, and the Mask of Paralysis appeared, just above my head, looking down on me.

It was without sex, which was part of its horror, and appeared to be made of crumpled white paper. It had a parrot nose, like Mr Punch in my puppet box, and nodded and smiled at me: and the smile wished me nothing but ill.

• From *The Doubleman*, C. J. Koch, p. 10.

155

The Doubleman is, among other things, about the spiritual battle between the forces of darkness and the forces of light. In this extract, the narrator is a young boy struck by polio. But this scene acts as a metaphor for that much larger design of the book: this scene could have been summed up in a sentence, but Koch has chosen to use it as a sustained metaphor for the issues that will follow in the rest of the book.

...

There were some non-committal but persistent cats; they were big and soft, with shiny fur. I woke the first night to find that one had hidden itself under the bed and now, in the dim light that filtered through the white paper blinds from the street, it silently repossessed the room. First the white-painted shelves by the windows, from which it stepped delicately onto the desk. It's nose poked inquisitively into a strange glass of water, and then at the keys of the antiquated Remington typewriter, borrowed for the duration. Someone else's papers. Then the shelves on the other side of the room, the spaces once filled with books and now almost empty. Finally the cane screen behind which I had hung my few clothes. The cat made its first sound here, as it sharpened its claws on the basket work.

When I got up and padded barefoot across the parquet floor to open the door and let it out, the cat ran back under the bed. After a while, as I continued to stand in the darkness, it trotted quickly to the black gap and disappeared.

In the daytime, the cats gazed from high shelves in other rooms of the apartment, or from dark cupboards with the doors ajar. I rarely saw them in motion, but their constant repositioning made them impossible to count. There were probably five, I thought. The one that came into my room, the little grey one, was called Constance.

In the morning when I opened the door to go to the bathroom, Constance often darted in and under the bed. The first time, I kneeled and flipped back the cotton bedspread printed with pink, yellow and blue spring flowers. Constance returned my gaze evenly, just out of reach. She yawned, and then in the narrow space rolled over onto her back, lolling with her paws outspread provocatively among the dust balls. I flipped the bed-spread down and went out, careful to leave the door open.

• • •

I lay in the bath, a little cramped in the narrow, fore-shortened porcelain tub. The bathroom was only as wide as the tub itself. At the other end was a narrow window which looked over to the neighbouring block of brick apartments. When I drew up my knees and sub-merged myself, the water level rose about two inches. Constance, the little grey cat, sat on the rim and looked at me. If I moved, she looked at whatever part of me moved. Then she looked back at my eyes. I began to feel a little self-conscious.

Constance adjusted her position on the rim and slid one paw down the inside of the bath. She hung her rear over the outside as a counterweight and then dipped her head. She started lapping while she was still some way above the surface of the water, her pink tongue appear-ing and disappearing, until slowly the little moving tongue hit the meniscus and scooped up minute amounts of warm water.

I had a sudden image of the bath emptying around me. I waited for her to fall in. But I did not move to push her off. When I got out of the bath I checked her drinking bowl to refill it. It was not empty, of course.

• From 'the Writing Class', in
After the Great Novelist and other stories,
Suzanne Falkiner, pp. 93, 103–104.

These two extracts are from a story about an Australian in New York: among other things it's a story about feeling foreign and about living in a space, literal and metaphoric, that isn't your own. That theme is given life by the image of the cats; the power of the image says it all, without explicit statements. In the first extract, at the start of the story, the cat repossesses the room in a way that announces that it is the cat, not the narrator, who belongs there. In the second extract, the cat is again establishing its rights, but this time in a way that could also be an overture of friendship.

The design of this story is based on images; there is an accumulation of various images, such as the cats, in which the condition of being foreign is explored in an oblique way.

•••

When Jimmie was taken from camp for his initiation, Dulcie Blacksmith presumed him dead for the time being. The epoch-old agenda of ceremonies was kept a secret from all the women. As far as Dulcie knew, the great lizard had mashed and swallowed him and would now give birth to him as a completed Mungindi man.

He was gone for weeks. The mission station superintendent, Rev. H. J. Neville, B. A., kept asking where Jimmie was but was not incommoded with any part of the truth.

Grown Mungindi men — Jackie Smolders for example — knew that Jimmie was hiding in the scrub close to an anabranch of the Macquarie River. Here he waited for the wound to heal and lived on possum meat. He was full of exhilaration of tribal manhood and the relief of finding that the lizard story was not true to the extent of his being actually chewed or swallowed.

•••

Ten days after Easter, Jimmie reappeared at Brentwood.

His half-sister, Bibra Dottie Blacksmith, was the first to notice his quiet entry. Then some other women and his half-brother Morton.

Dottie ran before him ululating in her high fifteen-year old voice:

'Born from the Lizard comes my· shining brother Tullam man.'

Morton woke Jimmie's presumptive father, Wilf Blacksmith, who was well on the way to death, only a few years away, by pneumonia and alcohol. Dulcie dropped a shirt of Wilf's that she had been washing in a basin in the sun. She shivered, for — with Jimmie's manhood accomplished — the cold weather had already set in.

Dulcie could see her son coming through the loose thicket where the hovels of Brentwood stood. The sun emphasized his funny pale hair. Men hooted his passage in a comradely way. Small children ran across his path. Piercing the day, Bibra Dottie's voice sang the news:

'Out of the monster's mouth, sealed in manhood, comes my Tullam brother.'

How Dulcie laughed! She and Morton laughed wildly on solemn occasions and Mr Neville therefore thought them dense. It was not the truth.

'Where yer bin, yer paley bastard?' Dulcie screamed in the crisp, Cockneyfied version of English that natives spoke. Still holding Wilf's irrelevant stained shirt she picked up the song from Dottie.

'Out of the Lizard's belly come my sons, crushing frost, making large marks on the earth, sons returning in manhood who were sucklings from my belly, born to Emu-Wren by me.'

Mr Neville had watched from his veranda the return of young Jimmie Blacksmith.

'Excitable people,' he murmured. 'Excitable people.'

It made him happy to see them. God must love those who greet mere absentees with so much ardour. It was as if the boy had come back from the dead.

Mr Neville wondered if, this once, he might get a sensible, explicit answer from a black. He walked down the path and out onto the dusty grass of the mission station.

'Jimmie Blacksmith!' he called. His voice cut the shrilling off. When Jimmie broke off his path and came towards the missioner, his brother Morton staggered about with the hilarity of it. But there was silence. Jimmie's feet could be heard padding the earth in their light economic way.

'Where have you been, Master Blacksmith?'

'Catchin' possums.'

Mr Neville flinched. 'I can't understand you. Didn't it occur to you you might be needed for higher things? The Easter choir perhaps?'

'How d'yer mean, Mr Neville?'

You've missed a lot of school.'

'Yair, Mr Neville.'

'Very well. You must come to my study, please.'

> • From *The Chant of Jimmie Blacksmith*,
> Thomas Keneally, pp. 2 and 5–6.

The Chant of Jimmie Blacksmith is about a boy who is half-Aboriginal and half-white, and the intolerable pressures this mix of cultures places on him. The book doesn't just describe the confusion of cultural messages: it acts them out so that the reader is saturated with a sense of both cultures operating simultaneously.

In the first extract, right at the beginning of the book, Jimmie's initiation ceremony is described. In the second extract, Jimmie returns to the mission into the full confusion of two cultures. Every other sentence reveals some incongruous mixing of Aboriginal and white cultures, from the two names of Jimmie's sister at the beginning, to the two totally different utterances Dulcie makes. Sentence by sentence, the reader experiences the incongruity and dividedness that Jimmie feels.

In the last few paragraphs we are given the experience of the white culture's response, and since we have been privy to the Aboriginal reasons for Jimmie's action, the response of the white culture seems ignorant and absurd. Within the first five pages of the novel, Keneally has taken the reader along a spectrum from Aboriginal culture (the initiation), through mixed cultures (the return), to white culture (Mr Neville's response). He has invited the reader to join in experiencing a sort of small-scale model of the entire book, and the cultural confusion it presents.

Exercises

T HE first step in designing a story is to get together a collection of events.

8.1 Take ten minutes to write an account of something you did yesterday. You might have climbed Everest or you might have made a cup of tea. It doesn't matter. Include as many different events, no matter how trivial, as you can, to give yourself plenty of material to work on.

The first step is to look at what you've got: the way your piece works on the level of event.
- Did you tell your events in strict chronological order or is there a point where you've darted backwards or forwards?
- Is there something in these events that you might call a 'climax'? Is there some event that all the others led up to? Or are all your events of equal weight, and just go along like beads on a string?
- Do you just have one string of events, or do you have more than one?
- Have you told another story in miniature, perhaps to explain something in yesterday's events? Have you referred to some past action, or some future hope?
- Is there a second character who creates a second ministory?

8.2 Now that you can see what you've got, try re-arranging it.
- If you have a strictly chronological piece, you could try putting the end at the beginning, or telling it backwards.
- If you have a climax, you could try to make it more climactic by streamlining everything else to make the climax more forceful.

- If you have several kinds of events or several characters or any references to past or future, you could try arranging the piece in a flashback structure or a story-within-a-story or as two parallel stories.
- Where your piece ends, ask the question 'and then what happened'. See if you can give the plot another twist.
- Invent new events and discard real ones as it suits your purposes. As an exercise, try to re-arrange the piece as differently as you can from the original way it was written, even if the original structure seems the best.

Next, look at your piece from the point of view of secrets: perhaps it can be made more interesting by concealing something.

- Is there something the narrator knows but isn't telling the reader?
- Is the narrator deliberately trying to mislead the reader?
- Is there something the reader knows that the narrator doesn't?
- Is there something that a character knows that they're not telling?
- At what point should information be given: should it all be laid out at the beginning or should information be withheld until the end?
- Is there something that should never be made quite clear, something that should stay obscure?

8.3 Re-write the piece with these questions in mind, arranging things so that something is concealed from someone.

Lastly, let's look at the focus of the piece. The first step, which is often the hardest, is to decide what the focus is.

8.4
- Give the piece a title, or several titles.
- Write a one-line summary of the piece.
- If you can, give the piece to someone else and ask

them to think of a title for the piece, or summarise it. Their way of seeing it may be quite surprising to you, and lead to new insights.

- Is there some unifying thread through all the events? Did they all happen to the same person, for example, or are they all tragic?
- Has anything been repeated in the piece: a word, a kind of action, a feeling, an image?

The answers to these questions will probably give you some idea about the focus of your piece. Now re-write it, sharpening the focus. Remove, or play down, anything that doesn't help to focus it, and invent anything you can to make the focus clearer.

The focus of a piece can change drastically as you explore it further. The initial focus may be rather thin and obvious, but further writing might give you a more complex focus. See if these shift the focus of your piece at all:

8.5
- Delete the first paragraph of your piece so that the second paragraph becomes the start of the piece. Does that suggest a different emphasis?
- Make the piece half as long. What have you left out?
- Make the piece twice as long. What have you added?

Building your story

B Y now it's very likely that you've written enough of your embryonic story that its basic design is taking shape.

Look at the material you have and consider whether this will be a story with a strong plot-line — plenty of different things happening, twists and surprises at every turn — or whether yours is a story with a minimal plot. Perhaps it's a deliberately plotless story, self-consciously going against the idea of a well-made plot.

Next, make a list of the events in the material you have. List them in whatever order you find them and include even very minor events.

If you seem to have too many events that don't go together, a great muddle of different things happening, try this. Draw up a time-line. Depending on the scale of your events, it might list the years of a decade, the days of a week, or the hours of a day. Now place each of your events where it might belong on this time-line. Start with the ones that have a very definite place and leave until last the events that could just as well take place at one time as another.

This ought to clarify what you have. You may see that you have several quite separate stories: you may be able to weave them together using the ideas for multi-story writing — flashback, subplot, parallel stories. Or you may see that you should choose one of these stories and put the others aside for the moment, perhaps for another story altogether.

If you have the opposite problem — not enough events to spin into a plot — try this. Go through all your pieces of writing looking for things that can be put together. One character could be put with another and give rise to an event — even a minor event such as a conversation or a walk together. A character could be put together with a landscape, or an object. A piece of dialogue could be put together with a room.

Another thing to try is to make a list of each piece of writing in the form of a one-phrase summary. Separate pieces of paper might help here. Try putting different elements of your list side-by-side and considering what you'd have to write in order to connect one element to the other.

Think about the few basic themes on which all other stories are variations: the quest story, the love story, the revenge story, the journey–of–self–discovery story, the rise–and–fall–of–power story, and so on. See if there are any parts of what you have that might fall into one of these categories. If so, think of an example of such a story — from myths, movies, books, or family lore — that appeals to you, and see if you can borrow its basic structure.

If you already have a fairly clear idea of your plot, see if it can be elaborated or made richer. Try this: write down a summary of the plot, with each event on a new line. Look at each line one by one and note all the directions the story could take from that point. Consider each line as a cross-roads with a great many possible directions. Some will be more obvious than others, some will be more plausible than others. Consider what you'd have to do to the story to make some of these directions possible. In doing so, you may see a possibility for more interesting directions that you'd thought of originally.

Try breaking your plot up and putting it together differently: reversing the beginning and the end, providing subplots or flashbacks, keeping something concealed.

See what happens if you make your story half as long or twice as long: what do you omit or add, and why?

Now you should have some kind of story line, or sequence of events.

Look through the material from the point of view of secrets. Is the narrator not telling the whole truth? Is there a character who doesn't know something? Is there something the reader hasn't been told? Is there something that you, the writer, don't know or don't understand in what you've got? If the answer to all these is 'yes', go through and see if there's anywhere you could introduce a dimension of secret to your story.

Look through the material for focus. Could you give the whole piece a title? Or could you give different sections of it different titles? Could you summarise it in one or two lines? Does a character keep recurring as the central figure? Is there a mood that recurs, or a voice?

Now assemble your material along the lines of the design that all this suggests to you. If the end of the story is clear but you're not sure how it will start, begin by writing out the end. Start with the parts you're most sure about and leave gaps in between if necessary. Expand where you need to and be ruthless about deleting. Keep a separate folder for the deletions — it makes it less painful to remove them if you know you've still got them and might use them in another story. You may find you need to re-write some sections several times before they work, while others don't need any changes at all. Work at this until you have a basic shape and structure, something that can be called a story.

However rough or however polished your story is now, revision is likely to improve it. That's what the next chapter will do.

9. Revision

What is revision?

Revision should be a complete re-vision. Revision looks at the overall shape and structure of the piece and considers radical changes. Revision isn't the same as editing: editing is the very last stage, the fine polishing and correcting of small details of word use, grammar and structure.

Knowing that you can revise as much as you like is what gives you the freedom to try anything. Trying anything, even things that seem unpromising, is a way to come up with writing that's original and full of energy.

How much should you revise?

Some writers revise a great deal: they might write a dozen or more drafts before they're happy. They may end up by returning to their first idea, but it will be enriched by the other drafts they've written. Many writers say that revision is the part of writing that they most enjoy: they've got the raw material and they can enjoy the process of transforming it continually until it's right.

Other writers revise very little, at least on the page. For such writers the revision process goes on in their heads so that by the time they come to write they've worked through various alternatives in their minds and can go straight to a finished version. My own feeling is if you're new to writing, revision will always improve your work. And apart from improving the finished product, revision is a way of exploring options that might turn out to be much more dynamic than the original ideas.

People sometimes talk of writing that's 'overworked', that's been re-worked and re-written in such a way that it's lost its original energy. Don't let the threat of overworking your piece prevent you from revising it. Two ways to make sure overworking doesn't happen are:

- Make sure that what you're doing is revision, not editing. That overworked feeling often comes when details have been tinkered with endlessly, but the basic ideas and structures haven't been changed.
- Be prepared to put a piece aside for a time and work on something else so that you can return to the first piece freshly. It often happens that, in writing another piece, you learn what you need to know in order to improve the original piece.

There's certainly a point where you reach a stalemate with a story. That doesn't always mean it's finished: it just means you've reached the limit of your present writing skill. When you've learned more, by writing more, you may then return and finish it.

When does revision come to an end? Only when it's too late to make any more changes: when the story is set in print.

Why revision is hard

The hardest thing about revision is being ruthless: crossing out a paragraph can feel like killing a friend. As already mentioned, one way to make it easier is not to throw anything away, but to put all your rejects into a folder of their own. Next time you're writing, you might be able to use some of them. In any case, it makes the surgery of revision less painful.

The other obstacle to revision is that it's hard to forget your original intention and to look at what you actually have. Your original intentions might have been brilliant but if what you actually have is something entirely different, there's not much point trying to force them together. Better to go with what you have and use the strengths of that.

It's not easy to come freshly to something you've written and read it as a first-time reader would, but that's what you need to be able to do to revise a piece. It's tempting to get around this by showing the piece to someone who's literally coming to it for the first time — a friend or family member. Sometimes this is useful, but it can also be counter-productive. For one thing, if you show it to ten different people, you'll have ten different ideas about how it should be rewritten. For another, friends and family mean well and may try to read a piece objectively but their relationship with you is the context of their reading. They may not like to tell you if it's awful, or they may not want to tell you if it's great. Above all, any reader brings to the piece his or her own ideas about what a piece of writing should offer. They may not be the same as your ideas. You're the only one who can know what your piece should be like: other people can only tell you the piece they would have written.

Pace

Pace is one of those things that you only recognise when it's missing. Pace is partly a matter of the speed at which things happen in a piece. Some first drafts hurtle along at a breakneck pace and might need to be slowed down with dialogue, description, detailed incidents, and so on. Other first drafts creep along so that the temptation is to skip until something gets moving. Slow first drafts may need a judicious injection of swiftly moving events and the introduction of new details.

But pace is also a matter of the order in which things happen and the language that's used. It can be that a single large block of event, or description, needs to be cut up and presented as several small sections. Events may need to be re-arranged so that they either flow more quickly or backtrack now and again to slow things down. Language may need to be streamlined to flow faster or elaborated on in order to linger a bit more. Syntax may need to be smoothed out or made more dense.

Pace is also a matter of having things happen at different speeds. Some parts of a story should move more quickly than others: variety is one of the keys to pace.

It's hard to be prescriptive about such a nebulous thing as

pace. But if you try some of the alternatives in the exercises in this chapter, you'll find that some versions have more 'pace' than others. Without trying to work out just what pace is, or just how to get it, you can keep it when it appears and keep trying until it does.

T HIS is the final version of the story that began as
the fragments in Chapter 2. I've written a lot of new
material, discarded some of the original ideas, and re-
arranged the order of events several times. I've worked on
the characters, decided (after a few false starts) on a point of
view, arrived at a voice that seems to suit that point of view,
and written some dialogue, though not much. In thinking
about the design of the piece, I found through several
intermediate drafts, the focus of the piece, found a way in
which I could introduce a secret, and worked out a very
small-scale plot or series of events on which to hang the
rest.

Between those fragments and this version there were
about six re-writes of varying degrees of radical change, and
a time-span of several months. I'm showing you the finished
version here not to make any great claims for this story, and
certainly not to suggest this is the way a story should look;
it's here only to demonstrate the distance between a first
conception and a finished product, and how even very
unpromising raw material can often find a way of becoming
useful in a story.

The piece, 'Look on my Works', was recently published in
the anthology, *Expressway*, edited by Helen Daniel (Penguin,
1989).

In the mottled old bar of a certain peeling old pub,
which I fancied for its mottled and peeling qualities, and
for the brass rail that just held your foot up nicely —
there was talk of it being knocked down to make way for
some bit of engineering or other, so I savoured the
mottled and peeling qualities and the brass rail all the
more for knowing they would soon be gone — in this bar
I met a traveller from an antique land.

The traveller was a man with a beer in his hand like
the rest of us, and I would not have spoken except that
my foot had struck his, and my elbow jogged his, as I

had presented myself at the bar, and having apologised it seemed the companiable thing to do to exchange a remark or two: all the more so since I myself was a man in a suit, while the traveller was a man in a jumper with egg down the front, and I did not want to be thought stand-offish. A man in a suit has an obligation to appear egalitarian. It must not be thought that he thinks his suit gives him any rights.

I stood, then, a hand around my beer, a foot nicely held up by the brass rail. On this particular evening I would have chosen to drink something more numbing than beer, something forgetful, something in a small glass, something to stop my heart dead in its tracks. But having jogged the jumper and established my democratic sentiments by apologising, I could not then drink anything but the peoples' drink. I snatched it up somewhat when it was slopped on the towel, for my hand was shaking, I observed: my pale hand trembled, and I did not wish any beer drinker in a jumper to notice and ask why.

He looked, I could feel him looking, and to throttle his words as they rose into his throat, I offered a remark about the weather. I could not remember the weather, I could not remember anything much: I could only think of a sort of limbo outside, neither day nor night, neither fine nor foul. However, being a person who believed in the social niceties, I knew what sort of remark a blue suit (arranged in its cutting and stitching so as to make little of a paunch) should offer a jumper with a ravelled sleeve and egg down the front: 'Funny old weather,' I said, 'Isn't it'.

One thing led to another, and after a small exchange of remarks, his vowels led me to ask where he was from. This is the way these things happen with the foam sliding down the side of the glass. 'And where would you be from, exactly, yourself?' I asked. He put down the beer, wiped his hands on his jumper, took his foot off the brass rail that had been holding it up nicely, and announced: 'I am from nowhere at all, mate. I am a traveller.' Then, shrugging as if bored with his own bombast, he added, 'From an antique land, a land that is out-of-date now.'

'Where, exactly?' I asked, for I was piqued not to be given a straight answer by this swarthy shifty thick-tongued fellow, making patterns on the floor with his shoe, a worn and soiled tennis-shoe that had probably never seen a tennis-court. Was he ashamed? or fabricating? 'Oh,' he cried when I insisted, and men near us turned, beers in hand, to stare.' Oh! There is no use telling you, my friend, you will not have heard its name, and it is on no map now.' He tossed back his beer as if it were some clear fiery liquor, and stared at me for a moment during which I wondered if he might fling the glass to the floor in a flamboyant Slavic gesture. I began to wish I had not spoken to this gent, who, I now observed, was as likely to be simply another reffo ratbag with a chip on his shoulder and garlic on his breath, as someone who might take my mind off things.

I wished now to change the subject and to quell other exclamations that I could see blossoming within the breast of the jumper: I had set him off, asking him where he was from, but I did not wish to hear about his history, or his travels, or his antique land. 'And what is your business, here in Australia?' I asked, not much wanting to hear about that either, but wishing to lead him into quieter waters. He did not hear my question the first time, and I repeated it carefully, making the word Australia sound as unantique, as prosaic and brick-and-tile as I could, and making my question quite devoid of any symbolic or grandiose possibilities.

The reffo ratbag, or traveller, looked gloomy. He had not smashed the glass at our feet, but now stood with it in his fist in such a gripe I expected to see it explode in his hand. 'Oh,' he said with a sniff and a wipe of his nose with the back of his hand. 'I am in the building racket'. He paused and flicked at the egg on his jumper. 'I am a brick-johnny. I hump the bloody bricks.' We were on steadier ground here, I thought, and hoped that after a remark or two about the slump, or the boom, or whatever was going on in the building racket—which might also remind this shabby person that a blue suit might only be making an effort to be polite, and not really wish a long conversation with a brick-johnny—I might be able to turn my back on him and set myself seriously to the business of drowning my sorrows.

But on the subject of bloody bricks this person was prepared to wax eloquent. 'Did you know,' he cried, 'how many bricks it takes to make up a wall? Did you know that bricks can sweat like flesh? Did you know that there is a hollow bubble of nothing in the heart of each and every brick?' He was excited again, and swelling within the green jumper: he came closer so that I could smell garlic and grout. 'I know these things. I know bricks backwards.'

Well, I am not a man to boast, and had no wish to set myself up in competition with this gent, but the fact is that I know a thing or two about bricks myself, and walls are something of an interest with me. If I had thought he knew, I would have asked this expert something that I had heard, and not known whether to believe: I had heard that if a person builds a wall high enough, the bricks at the bottom begin to run like putty under the pressure. I would like to build such a colossal wall, and see bricks turn to water.

However, small walls have been my destiny: I have built many small walls in my time. Walls are something I find soothing, and building another wall is a way of not being in the house. My wife, inside the house, behind her walls, is a good wife, but she does not meet my eye: she does not warm me with looks, nor yet with flesh.

A wall is a good work. I have made walls of bricks, and find it hard to believe that such a substantial item as a brick could be hollow as this man says. I have made walls of stone, flat slabs laid on their end, or chunks fitted in among each other: I have built walls of masonry blocks, I have built walls of rubble and faced them with fragments of marble and coloured stone. Ours is a garden of small walls, of walls within walls. The outer wall is my greatest monument: it is a sort of sampler of the brick-layer's art, with offset corners, edge-work coping, and a pair of fine blocks beside the gate on which lions would squat if ours were that sort of street.

'Churchill built walls,' I announced, rather more loudly than I had intended, in order to break into the traveller's flow of speech, for he was still speaking of the bricks and buildings he knew backwards. The traveller was taken by surprise and fell silent: for a moment I felt myself to be a great singer in some opera, and the chorus had fallen silent so that I could sing my aria. But before I could sing—and besides, I had nothing more to say, or sing, on the subject of Winston Churchill and his walls—the man on the other side of me, another man in a suit, turned around and said, 'Yes, and he won the bloody war, mate, beat the bloody Krauts,' and laughed with a look of contempt at the egg-stain and the ragged tennis-shoes, and turned back to his conversation. He was one of those men who know what is what, about Winston Churchill, or walls, or any other subject you might care to name, a man quite sure of his facts, a man who knew he was going to Heaven, and in the meantime he would put anyone right about any fact they might doubt.

I was not such a man, not a man certain of the world, not a man sure of his facts, not a man sure of Heaven: just a brick in a suit with a hollow bubble at my heart.

I had set this traveller in motion, and it was now beyond my power to stop him: he was determined to tell me all. And I did not mind listening: none of these other beer drinkers, in their suits and certainties, could send the warm shaft of a word into the heart of my fear, but this man, who had seen so much, and whose head was full of some other tongue altogether, might. So I listened, although askance, as befitted a blue suit who had set off the clockwork mystery of a talkative foreign gent.

'I have seen the seven wonderful things,' the traveller said, and the blue suit automatically put him right: 'The seven wonders of the world, you mean.' 'Yes!' he exclaimed, 'Yes! You know what I mean. I have seen the pyramids.' He thought, and his eyes narrowed. 'But I would not sit down on them, because the priests mixed smallpox into the mortar, did you know that?' He stared at me, his eyes dark, and I saw the skull beneath the skin: then he set the skull into motion again with words, which made it once again a face: 'Babylon is in small pieces, in glass boxes, in a museum that is always closed for lunch.' He laughed so I saw his mouthful of gold molars, and he scratched his chest with the pleasure of his wit: 'Babylon is closed for lunch.'

'Pisa, oh,' he waved contemptuously. 'It is short, not tall, and nothing interesting except crooked.' He shrugged. 'Not wonderful, and around the base, you read the signs'—he spread his hand around against the air so the powdered cleavage turned his way, thinking he wanted another beer—'all in a row, Coca-Cola, Pepsi, Marlboro, Macdonald's, Esso.' He looked into his beer, dismissing Pisa from him, but I was interested

175

now, and said, 'And the Great Wall? Have you seen the Great Wall?'

He took a while to answer so that when he did I did not believe him, but I listened in any case. A lifetime of truth had been no help to me, so I would listen to a moment of something that was an invention. 'Oh yes,' he said. 'It is in ruins, you know.' He met my eye insistently, filled with a liar's conviction. 'There are two vast' — he gestured vaguely, stuck for words. 'Towers,' he said at last, 'two towers like a pair of pants. And there is a small bit of wall in between. Around is all decay, things half sunk back into the dirt, God knows what!' He was becoming indignant at his picture of the Wall now, but I nodded to egg him on, it was soothing me to hear of these wonderful shattered things. 'All around' — he made a level horizon gesture with his hand — 'bare like a table, level like a table, not a soul, not a twig, just the sand, it is all wreck, what they thought would be forever.'

I was running through the seven wonders trying to remember the others, but he shifted now and called for beer. He was ready for a change of pace and put his hand rather suddenly on the blue arm next to him, my own arm. 'Listen,' he hissed, 'There was a time when I would have been shot for this,' and he began to sing, in a strong voice that wavered with sincerity. It was of course a foreign song, with no words I knew, but with noble sentiments that brought his hand to the green jumper over his heart. It went on for some time, a sad sort of tune sighing up and down, turning over the words of the foreign tongue the way a stream turns over pebbles. The traveller stood at attention as he sang, his large dark eyes glittered with tears, and the muscles of his neck stood out powerfully beneath the skin.

I was mortified, the way everyone was turning to look, and the powdered cleavage looking dubious and hovering near the hatchway, in case Jack the publican would have to be called: I was mortified by so many eyes seeing that it was I who had incited this man to make a spectacle of himself, and bring the sounds of fir forests and wolves into this place of placid gentlemen in hats exchanging a remark or two.

I was mortified, but at last I was drawn down past my mortification: this sighing song drew me along with it so that I could see those dark fir forests, those wolves snuffing after lambs, those castles of cold stone, those smoking peat-fires in humble rooms where soup and rough bread waited in wooden bowls. And although the traveller was still a man whose chest swelled beneath an egg-stained jumper, he was also a man in cossack braid, a man in gypsy tatters, a man in homespun with the mud of his furrows on his boots, a man with waxed moustaches and velvet facings on the top of a prancing horse.

When the singing stopped, we all turned into our glasses to tide us over the moment. The singer took a long swallow, only himself again now. 'I was beaten for that,' he said. 'In the war—you, here, were safe—in the war I was beaten and burned for singing that song, my homeland's song, the song of my people. And I will tell you this, my friend,' he said, and thumped his fist on the bar so an ashtray jumped, 'I would remember his face anywhere, the way he sneered as he beat me, yes, I would know him now.' He glanced around the bar, but there was no sneering here, only lips pursing towards the rims of their glasses.

'And you, mate,' the traveller said, 'what is your past, tell me.' I spoke without care, and found that I had said 'I have no past, I am dying,' when I knew that it is the future that the dying lack, not the past. But it did not matter, this man was not a close listener. 'Oh, mate, we are all dying,' he exclaimed, as if it was easy. 'We are all dying every minute, mate, why, I myself am dying!' He laughed, it was a fine joke, and stood back to make a show of looking me up and down. 'You are a man behind a desk, mate, am I right?' he asked, but did not wait for me to say Yes or No or to tell him what kind of bits of paper were on the desk, he in the blindness of life was rushing on: 'Mate, you have it easy, but I do not complain, I am alive after the beatings, my country is gone but I am not.'

What a smile he gave me then! I saw him in his smile: I saw that he was a man who would never completely die. He was a man who would live to a hundred, a man who had a song, which he would teach to his grand-children, and make sure they remembered it right. He would make them sing it when he saw them, and then make them laugh with rabbit's ears on the wall, and the way he could make his cheeks go inside-out: they would laugh, and not forget, and make sure their own children learned that song, and how to sing it standing at attention, with a hand on the heart.

He was a man who would have plenty of faces at his funeral, and later there would be plenty of fiery liquor in small glasses that would be smashed, and there would be plenty of friends, countrymen and family to shout his name in heat as the glasses shattered. And those grandchildren, sweet and dark, serious in their funeral best, would be called on to sing the song of his lost country which he had taught them, and all the friends and countrymen and family would grow wistful, tearful, melancholy in a proud glad way, weeping for their vanished nation as well as their freshly buried friend.

Talking to this soiled foreigner, I felt myself no longer part of the world that knew what was what about Winston Churchill and walls. I was joining the world about which those others exchanged glances and winked. I, who would never have dreamt of allowing an egg-stained foreign ratbag to sing his national anthem to me, much less joined in conversation with him on the subject of the Seven Wonderful Things, had now slid beyond some wall or other. I was outside now, I was joining the greatest ratbaggery of all, the ratbaggery of death.

My mind turned to the things that would remain after me, after my time. When my suit was hung for the last time, what else would there be? I have no songs. I have, in addition to this blue suit, a rectangle of earth, on which there is a lawn and a house and a great many small walls. There are no dandelions in my lawn, no oxalis in my borders, and no aphis on my roses. There are no leaves in my gutters, for in my suburb we do not allow our vegetation to reach higher than a man. I have a wife who will make an appropriate widow, and four pairs of shoes, size ten.

My shoes will be worn by some gent down on his luck in a dosshouse, some other lucky ratbag will make the pockets of this suit bulge with his bottle: oxalis and aphis and dandelions will take root in my lawn, my borders, my roses: and my walls will crumble, slowly, back into the dirt.

A dullness is stealing over me now: I am sick of this

histrionic traveller with his tall tales and songs, who will live when I will not. This traveller fills me with longing for how little I have that I could weep over losing. Now a screaming is beginning to swell in my head, and each object in front of me grows a small dark halo. Silence swells around me like a stain and I am afraid. It is dark behind my eyes, my fingers are numb, my body is becoming blind to itself. Somewhere beneath where I stand, I can hear a slow shovel scraping at earth: it is not in any hurry, but it will not stop until it has scraped into the earth, deep enough to make a hole fit for a man.

- From 'Look on my Works', Kate Grenville, in *Expressway*, pp. 101–108.

Finishing your story

TAKE the first draft of your story from the previous chapter. First, try to find the central core of your story: where its heart lies.

Read it through swiftly and write down what you think the centre of interest of the story is. A character, the events, the language? Go through and mark the parts of the story that you think are working and the parts that don't feel right. Find on each page the phrase or sentence you like best — for whatever reason.

Tell the bare bones of the plot in a few lines. What does this leave out, that seems important? Are there any elements of the story that you don't actually need, but which you like? It's possible that those elements are what the story should really be about.

It's not too late for a radical shift in the centre of your story; the important thing is to locate its strengths and follow them up. Now that you've isolated the core and strengths of your story, re-write it from memory, without looking at the original. This is a good way to get a new perspective on it and to discover afresh what you are drawn to in the story.

Now that you've worked on the overall shape, you can focus on the different aspects of a story — character, point of view, dialogue, etc. — that you've worked through in the course of the book.

By this stage, the different aspects will be meshing together and it will be harder to consider them separately. Be very flexible: start with whichever aspect seems to be working best and work out from there. Weave backwards and forwards: as you make a change in one area, you may have to go back and re-think another.

In revising, you don't have to start at the beginning of the story each time and work through to the end. Sometimes it's best to start with the strongest part of the story and work outwards from it. Sometimes it's good to start with the weakest part and concentrate on that until it's starting to work. Other times you need to start with the end of the story, where it's faded away, and work on it to make it as dynamic as the beginning. You might have to try a dozen different ways of starting the story before you arrive at the best one.

But at some point in your revising, consider each of the following aspects.

The characters

What is each one doing in the story? Are some of them unnecessary, perhaps left over from when your story was drawn from real life? Would some of them be better combined into one character? Are you asking one character to carry too much of the burden in the story: should you invent another character to share the load?

Are they drawn as individuals, or are they all faceless and the same? Can you make them more idiosyncratic, either by inventing qualities for them, or by borrowing a few quirks from real people?

Are they all equally likable, or all equally unpleasant? Would the story benefit from a greater variety?

Should the story focus more closely on one character, so that the reader has one character in the foreground while the rest are less significant background figures? Or should some background characters be brought up into closer focus?

Sometimes drawing a family tree for your characters will suggest new ideas: sometimes a short biography for each character will help. Neither will necessarily go into the finished story.

If your characters have names, are they the best they could have or were they just the first names you thought of? Should ordinary characters always have ordinary names? Should exotic characters always have exotic names? You can look in the phone book to get ideas for names and also in the dictionary: ordinary words often make very striking names that can underscore something about the character.

Point of view

Who is telling your story? How much do they know? Are they telling the truth?

Consider all the possible points of view for your story, including unlikely ones. Consider the full range, from an impersonal third-person point of view to a very subjective first-person point of view. Consider all your characters one by one as candidates for the point of view. Think about which point of view is very clear but perhaps rather dull, and what points of view might be more oblique but perhaps more intriguing.

The voice

The decision you make about the point of view will affect the voice or style of your story. Write a paragraph describing your narrator, then see whether the voice of the story really suits that narrator. Should the voice of the story be like a speaking voice, informal and easy-going? Or should it be a more 'literary' voice? Should the voice of the story be a very emotive one, or more impartial?

Experiment with different syntax, cutting up long sentences, or joining up short ones, or constructing very elaborate ones.

Experiment with different ways of punctuating the piece: try using only commas and full stops, then try adding colons, semi-colons, exclamation marks, etc., to see what works best.

See what difference it makes to the story if you change the tense.

Look at the details of word use: go through the piece looking at each verb. Are there more vivid verbs you could use that would enliven the writing? Or do very plain verbs work best for this story? Go through looking at where you've used adjectives and adverbs. Can you replace some of these with action or an image?

Dialogue

If there is none, go through looking for scenes that might be made more dramatic by adding dialogue. If you've used dialogue, should it be broken up into smaller sections separated by narrative? Or should it be joined up into a sustained exchange? Would indirect dialogue be more effective in some places?

Are the attributions clumsy, or discreet? If you're using realistic dialogue, does it sound right? Are the speakers too correct, too long-winded or too high-flown to be convincing?

Have you chosen punctuation that best indicates the music of the speech you want to get across? Read it aloud, imagining yourself seeing it for the first time.

Description
Are there descriptions in the story at the moment? If not, is there something that could be enhanced by being described? Might description have the effect of slowing down a runaway story or focusing attention on something significant?

If there are descriptions, are they just informative or do they have another dimension? Do they reveal something about the narrator? Are they interesting or amusing in themselves?

Go through your story and see where you might add the five senses so that it becomes a story full of smells and tastes and touches, as well as sounds and sights.

Design
Is there a more dramatic way of ordering and arranging the events? Remember all the possibilities of starting with the end, using flashbacks and sub-plots and so on. At the end of your story, what might happen next? What happened before the beginning of your story?

Is there any information you've assumed (about the sex or age of the narrator, for example), but forgotten to tell the reader about?

Can you introduce some secret into the story: some aspect of the story that's hidden from someone? Can you enhance the focus of the story by using imagery, symbolism, repetition, and so on?

Think of a story you like, written by someone else, and re-shape your own story so that it models itself on that other story. You might follow the syntax sentence by sentence or imitate the style or borrow its plot or structure.

Go through your story and find places where you've 'told' rather than 'shown'. Consider whether the story would be more interesting if it were re-written so that information was acted out rather than summed up.

Find a place in your story where you've described things in general terms—'every day, she was late for the bus'—and consider re-writing it as an event in present time.

All these are only guidelines. In the end, it's your story, and you must write it in the way that feels right to you. What feels right to you, though, is often the influence that other stories have had on you. There's nothing wrong with those influences, but the best way to discover what's unique about your stories, while still keeping the best of the influences, is to try many different approaches when revising. A story only reveals itself by being written, not by being thought about in the abstract. If you're circling around your story by trying different ways of writing it, it may seem an indirect way of getting there, but it might be quickest in the end.

Keep revising until you feel you've explored everything you can. Then put the story aside for a week or a month and come back to it later. Then, if you're still happy with it, you can put it to the test and send it out for publication.

10. Submitting a manuscript

Why publish?

I T's a very natural impulse to show something you've made to other people and, when that thing happens to be a story, the craving for response is very great. In the course of writing a story you will have made discoveries, come across ideas or insights or odd quirks of behaviour that are new to you, and exhilarating. Sharing that pleasure with readers makes it all the greater.

Wanting to share something you've made seems to me a good reason for wishing to be published. But before you send your story off, consider the possibility that it will be rejected: will that discourage you from writing another story? If the answer is yes, then resist the temptation to send it away. It's rare for a writer's first story to be published: even their twenty-first story may be rejected. Rejection slips are nasty, cold little things and have a dampening effect on the spirit. There seems no point in dampening the flame of your creativity before it's had a chance to start burning properly. So unless you're sure that even the curtest rejection slip won't stop you writing, wait awhile before you send anything out.

There are other, less innocent reasons for wanting to be published. It's sometimes thought that fame follows on from publishing. It's sometimes thought that being published means making a great deal of money. The search for fame and fortune are not good reasons for getting published, mainly because publication seldom brings either. For every best-selling writer forced to live on Norfolk Island because of her tax problem, there are hundreds of writers, including established ones, who can't make a living from their writing.

However, if you're serious about writing, the day will come when you feel you must send something out and find out whether you're writing for anyone besides yourself. When that day comes, keep this image in mind:

The publisher's desk

Whether the publisher is the editor of a small literary magazine, the editor of a mass-circulation magazine or the editor of a major book-publishing house, his or her desk will be overflowing with manuscripts. Dozens more arrive every week and the flow never stops. The editor knows from experience that, statistically, something like one manuscript in a hundred will be publishable. That means that your manuscript is up against fierce competition and it also means that the editor is in a hurry. If anything about a manuscript makes it a problem to read, it won't be read. So you must do everything you can to make the physical presentation of the manuscript as easy to read as possible. Once that hurdle is past, the editor can assess its literary worth.

Physical presentation for stories and novels

The manuscript must be typed in double space, on one side of the paper, with generous margins all round.

Every page must be numbered and if you are sending individual stories, write your surname in the top right-hand corner of every page, in case your story and a hundred others all spill off that desk. Fasten the pages together with a paper-clip. Don't use pins as a bleeding thumb will stand between an editor and the proper appreciation of your story. For longer pieces and novels, put the pages loose into a folder and hold it together with a giant rubber band, or have them bound with spiral-type binding.

Photocopies are fine as long as they are clear.

Give the manuscript a title page containing the title of the piece, its approximate word length, your name and address, and a copyright line. If you have a novel, you could also include a one-page synopsis, but this isn't essential.

Don't bother to write the editor a letter unless you have information that might affect his or her decision: a letter is one more thing for the editor to deal with. If your work has been previously published, however, or if you're nine years old, or if there's some other factor that the editor should know, it's worth mentioning in a very short note.

Make sure there are no unintentional spelling or grammar errors and if your typing is very poor, consider employing a typist.

Don't send more than three stories at any one time to the same editor.

Protecting your work

The most vitally important protection of all is to KEEP A COPY. Many terrible things happen on editors' desks and even more terrible things happen when editors take manuscripts home with them on the bus.

Protect yourself from endless suspense: unless you send a stamped, self-addressed envelope of the right size, you won't get your manuscript back and you probably won't get a response of any kind.

Protect yourself against plagiarism of your work by writing the copyright symbol, followed by your name, at the end of the piece.

Protect yourself from muddles by keeping accurate records of which stories you've sent to which publishers. If the editor rejected it the first time, it's likely to get thrown out the window the second time.

Protect yourself from contractual problems. If you have a story accepted, the editor will write an acceptance letter which should mention the rate of payment, if any, and should also include an indication of when the story is likely to appear. A year after the story has been published, you are entitled to submit it to other publications; this is what 'first serial rights' means. But if you do so, you must mention that the story has already been published.

If you have a book-length manuscript accepted, the publishers will ask you to sign a contract. It's important that you have this contract checked by someone qualified. The Australian Society of Authors runs a Contract Advisory Service for a small fee. Most publishers will offer an acceptable contract but you can't depend on yours being one of those publishers.

Will it be read?

Publishers are in business because they want to find work they can publish, so every manuscript is looked at, although not every manuscript is read all the way through.

The exception is mass-circulation magazines, the kind on sale in newsagents, which carry on their masthead page the warning that unsolicited manuscripts are not considered. This means that these magazines get their writing from commissioning writers or through literary agents. Save your postage with those and don't bother.

Agents

In Australia it's not essential to have an agent, although it's a good idea once you've had a few stories published or if you have a book accepted. Agents find publishers, negotiate terms with them and sometimes, not always, offer editorial advice on your work. They take 10 per cent of what you make from writing.

It's sometimes comforting to think that getting published is a matter of knowing the right people: such a theory can take the sting out of a rejection slip. Knowing the right people might ensure that your piece gets more than a cursory reading but, after that, it's still on its own. Publishers want and need to find good writing, otherwise they're out of business, and publishers know that good writing often comes without any important friends.

Where to send it?

In Australia, there aren't all that many outlets for short stories. There are a dozen literary magazines, there are a few regular collections of short stories and, irregularly, there are literary supplements in the weekend sections of newspapers. Spend some time in your local library getting the addresses, then send pieces systematically to them.

Short-story competitions are advertised in the literary pages of newspapers and also in the newsletter of the Australian Society of Authors. Sometimes local papers or special-interest magazines publish short fiction. Student magazines at universities or CAEs are an excellent place to start publishing fiction: you generally don't have to be a student to submit work.

If you have a book-length manuscript—a collection of stories or a novel—it's worth spending some time in the library getting a rough idea of which publishing houses publish what sort of books. Some specialise in textbooks, some in children's books, others in non-fiction, so you can narrow the field. Unless you have some special reason not to, you should pick a publisher with an Australian branch, or an Australian publisher (a fairly rare species), because they're more likely to be receptive to an Australian book and you avoid the delays and difficulties of overseas postage. Once you've found a publisher here, it may then be easier to sell rights overseas.

As well as this kind of 'mainstream' publishing, there is also a small group of alternative or independent publishers. They can serve a special-interest group—for example, the different small presses run for and by women—or they can simply operate as an alternative to the big, international publishing houses. They publish small numbers of books and sometimes find it difficult to have their books reviewed and stocked by libraries and bookshops. Sometimes, though, they also have runaway best-sellers, such as several of the Fremantle Arts Centre Press books.

These small presses are not to be confused with vanity presses. The way you can tell the difference is that with a vanity press, the writer pays the publisher, not the other way around. Journals don't review vanity press books and bookshops and libraries hardly ever stock them, so unless you have a large market that you yourself can sell to, you're likely to end up with 5000 copies of your book in your garage.

The money side

There's not much of this. Literary magazines pay a couple

of hundred dollars at the most for a story. Some pay much less. The money from a book comes in the form of royalties —the more copies you sell, the more money you make. As a rough guide, royalties on a paperback book are around 10 per cent of the cover price. You have to sell huge numbers to make serious money. It's hard to sell those huge numbers in Australia because our population is so small, so, without good overseas sales, a novel will not make its writer much money.

The bottom line

The bottom line about writing fiction is that it ought to be exhilarating, as well as perhaps frustrating. The world has enough books and enough writers already, so unless you find writing satisfying you might as well do something else. Writing is often called a craft, and it is. But the more important dimension of writing is that it's an art—it's part of the complex, slippery, subjective area where the human mind is out on the edge of experience, exploring new territory. It's not a mechanical matter of following rules and getting all the words in the right places. That's why readers disagree about books and it's why the process of writing is so fascinating.

If you want to write, there are only two things you must do. Firstly, you have to write and re-write, as regularly as you can, in whatever circumstances your life allows. Secondly, you have to read as widely as you can—not just books you like and feel comfortable with, but books you dislike, books that are difficult or frustrating to read, books that are unsettling. Read old books as well as new books, experimental books as well as traditional ones, biographies and non-fiction as well as novels, books in translation as well as books in English. The more you read, the better you'll write.

Bibliography

Adams, Glenda (1987) *Dancing on Coral* Sydney: Angus & Robertson
Anderson, Jessica (1980) *Tirra Lirra by the River* Melbourne: Penguin
Astley, Thea (1983) *A Boatload of Home Folk* Melbourne: Penguin
Bail, Murray (1975) 'The Drover's Wife' in *The Drover's Wife and other stories* Brisbane: University of Queensland Press
Bedford, Jean (1985) 'Isabella' in *Country Girl Again* Melbourne: McPhee Gribble/Penguin
Bird, Carmel (1987) 'Buttercup and Wendy' in *The Woodpecker Toy Fact and other stories* Melbourne: McPhee Gribble/Penguin
Campbell, Marion (1985) *Lines of Flight* Fremantle: Fremantle Arts Centre Press
Carey, Peter (1981) *Bliss* London: Picador
Carey, Peter (1985) *Illywhacker* Brisbane: University of Queensland Press
Coombs, Margaret (1988) *Regards to the Czar* Brisbane: University of Queensland Press
Couani, Anna (1986) 'Xmas in the Bush' in *Transgressions* ed. Don Anderson, Melbourne: Penguin
Dickins, Barry (1981) 'To the Beach Then, eh?' in *The Gift of the Gab* Melbourne: McPhee Gribble
Drewe, Robert (1983) 'The View from the Sandhills' in *The Bodysurfers* Sydney: James Fraser
Falkiner, Suzanne (1989) 'The Writing Class' in *After the Great Novelist and other stories* Sydney: Picador
Farmer, Beverley (1985) 'A Woman with Black Hair' in *Home Time* Melbourne: McPhee Gribble/Penguin
Foster, David (1987) *Testostero* Melbourne: Penguin
Garner, Helen (1984) *The Children's Bach* Melbourne: McPhee Gribble

Hanrahan, Barbara (1980) *The Frangipani Gardens* Brisbane: University of Queensland Press

Harper, Graeme (1988) *Black Cat, Green Field* Sydney: Black Swan Books

Harrower, Elizabeth (1966) *The Watch Tower* London: Macmillan

Hazzard, Shirley (1980) *The Transit of Venus* London: Penguin

Ireland, David (1981) *City of Women* Melbourne: Allen Lane

Jolley, Elizabeth (1983) *Mr Scobie's Riddle* Melbourne: Penguin

Krauth, Nigel (1983) *Matilda, My Darling* Sydney: Allen & Unwin

Keneally, Thomas (1979) *The Chant of Jimmy Blacksmith* Sydney: Angus & Robertson

Koch, C.J. (1985) *The Doubleman* Sydney: Australian Publishing Company

Lette, Kathy and Gabrielle Carey (1981) *Puberty Blues* Melbourne: McPhee Gribble

London, Joan (1986) 'Sister Ships' in *Sister Ships and other stories* Fremantle: Fremantle Arts Centre Press

Lunn, Richard (1986) 'Mirrors' in *Transgressions* ed. Don Anderson, Melbourne: Penguin

Malouf, David (1975) *Johnno* Brisbane: University of Queensland Press

Maniaty, Tony (1984) *The Children Must Dance* Melbourne: Penguin

Masters, Olga (1982) 'The Home Girls' in *The Home Girls* Brisbane: University of Queensland Press

Moorhead, Finola (1985) 'Waiting for Colombo' in *Room to Move* ed. Suzanne Falkiner, Sydney: Allen & Unwin

Moorhouse, Frank (1976) *Conference-ville* Sydney: Angus & Robertson

Murnane, Gerald (1988) 'The Only Adam' in *The Faber Book of Contemporary Australian Short Stories* London: Faber and Faber

Stead, Christina (1983) *For Love Alone* Sydney: Angus & Robertson

Walwicz, Ania (1986) 'Neons' in *Transgressions* ed. Don Anderson, Melbourne: Penguin

White, Patrick (1964) *Riders in the Chariot* London: Penguin

Windsor, Gerard (1985) 'Reasons for Going into Gynaecology' from *Memories of the Assassination Attempt and other stories* Melbourne: Penguin

Winton, Tim (1987) 'Distant Lands' in *Minimum of Two* Melbourne: McPhee Gribble/Penguin

Woolfe, Sue (1989) *Painted Woman* Melbourne: Hudson